D0717132

Hermann Aschwer

TIPS FOR SUCCESS
TRIATHLON

Meyer & Meyer Sport

Original title: Tipps für Triathlon
2. Auflage
– Aachen: Meyer und Meyer Verlag, 2000
Translated by Anne Lammert

British Library Cataloguing in Publication Data
A catalogue for this book is available from the British Library

Aschwer, Hermann:
Tips for Success-Triathlon/Hermann Aschwer
[Transl.: Anne Lammert].
– Oxford : Meyer & Meyer Sport (UK) Ltd., 2001
ISBN 1-84126-029-0

© 2001 by Meyer & Meyer Sport (UK) Ltd.
Oxford, Aachen, Olten (CH), Vienna, Québec,
Lansing/Michigan, Adelaide, Auckland, Johannesburg, Budapest
Member of the World

 Sportpublishers' Association
www.w-s-p-a.org

Cover Photo: Bongarts Sportfotografie GmbH, Hamburg
Photos: see list of photographs, p.102
Illustrations: Hermann Aschwer
Cover design: Birgit Engelen, Stolberg
Cover and type exposure: frw, Reiner Wahlen, Aachen
Editorial: John Coghlan, Jürgen Schiffer
Printed and bound in Germany
by Burgverlag Gastinger GmbH, Stolberg
ISBN 1-84126-029-0
e-mail: verlag@meyer-meyer-sports.com
www.meyer-meyer-sports.com

List of Contents   Page

Throughout this book, the pronouns he, she, him, her and so on are interchangeable and intended to be inclusive of both men and women. It is important in sport, as elsewhere, that men and women have equal status and opportunities.

Foreword

"Most people prefer taking the lift up to success to using the stairs", a typical quote of Hermann's. My friend Hermann is still climbing those steps to those meaningful steps for life. Even though he could have been taking the lift with pride and satisfaction a long time now.

"Look back and smell the roses" is what I would like to call out to Hermann. But he has no time for that. He takes time out for his beloved family, friends, his career, for triathlon - both actively and through his writings. In his prized dissertation Hermann focuses on a person's ability to take action - "it is easier to see the action than the idea, but it is the latter which triggers the action off". In this remarkable book Hermann describes the basic requirements for success-oriented action. Only by looking at something in its entirety can one achieve success - not only in sport. I, for my part, will never forget that Hermann, through his first book "My Adventure -Hawaii Triathlon" was the real motivation for my actions.

Whether or not he will have the same effect ON YOU depends entirely on yourself, but with this book in your hands you are also holding the key.

Prof. Georg Kroeger
Hawaii Finisher 87/88/ 89

1 Preface

Triathlon - this magical word has been haunting me since the early eighties when the first press and TV reports about an incredible competition from that island of dreams, Hawaii, reached us here in Germany. Over there in Hawaii, on the other side of the world, there were athletes covering inconceivable distances: a 3.86 km swim in the ocean, a 180.2 km cycle and then an entire marathon run of 42.195 km. Nearly impossible to believe given the extremely hot, humid and windy weather conditions over there.

As my regular marathon training at that time was becoming too monotonous I was on the look out for a new challenge. I tried my luck with triathlon. After my first triathlon competitions covering 1-2 km swimming, 40-70 km cycling and 10-15 km running a passion awakened within me, a passion which is shared today by hundreds of thousands of athletes in Germany alone. And a passion which gradually roused a dream from within - the dream of Hawaii. I adapted my plain running training and from then on I began a more varied and all round form of training in order to come a bit nearer to my target 'Hawaii'. Since then I have indeed competed several times in Hawaii, completed the Ironman Distance 20 times, even the Double Ironman Distance once, and have taken part in 120 triathlon competitions. The dreams which came true, the numerous positive experiences and fascinating adventures related to this sport, have had a deep impact on me.

The conseqences of my participation in triathlon in the last fifteen years have been so brilliant that I would very much like to pass on the practical experience which I have gained along with the theoretical knowledge and the background, not to mention the personal impressions, feelings and emotions.

Whoever organizes their training to concentrate on three forms of endurance sports will see a number of positive health aspects in their own body. Every person in training who from season to season first of all attains a basic endurance level, and only increases the intensity in the individual sports after the advanced level is reached, will be twice as successful in triathlon. He will firstly become a successful athlete working within his own limits, and furthermore his physical and mental well-being will benefit from this enormously. The proof that these important aspects can not only be reached through mindless, monotonous training with little attachment to fun, are the many good-humoured triathletes in training as well in competition.

The name of one of the best woman triathletes springs to mind here ahead of all the others - Natascha Badmann from Switzerland, world champion in duathlon and second in the Hawaii Ironman of 1996, who is such a nice person and always in a good mood in competitions. Like many others she was prompted through my books to take up triathlon, and she is the absolute proof that even at world class, triathlon can be fun and fun-oriented. Natascha Badmann wrote to me: "When I read your book I didn't dare dream that I would ever manage the Hawaii distances."

I would like to carry on taking you through these ventures, and the associated adventures, and assisting you with my hints and suggestions so that you can reach your personally set target.
In the "triathlon cycle" I would like to explain the entire structure of the triathlon competition. This includes the development and the complete order of events in a triathlon competition.

Before I begin let me pose the following question. Why do these three endurance activities swimming, cycling and running have such a strong magnetic attraction in an age so marked by lack of exercise?

There are certainly many explanations and answers to this. A very significant factor is the positive physical effect on heart, circulation, breathing and metabolism. A further motive behind the popularity of endurance sports applies for those endurance sportsmen whose focus lies in competition and performance. To want to compare oneself with others has been man's instinct since the beginning of time. This fact does not even lose its appeal when in a competition fitness athletes - who only train 3-4 hours a week-, and world-class athletes - who as professionals would train 30-40 hours a week-, come together to the start and try and use up their personal performance potential.

These two factors can generally be achieved together through balanced training. The rule here is to make as few mistakes as possible, or as much right as possible. Triathlon training must be in tune with individual factors, with personal requirements, possibilities and aims in order to reap the numerous positive aspects of endurance sports.

Finally some practical advice.

For reader-friendly reasons, the form of address refers to both sexes in this book.

As this book supplements my previous books I will refer to these writings at certain stages to avoid having to repeat myself.

As before I am still available to answer questions on triathlon which my many readers may have, and I am ever grateful for any ideas.

My address:
Dr. Hermann Aschwer, Ameke 40, 48317 Drensteinfurt

2 Triathlon - the Fitness Sport

Triathlon, made up of the three endurances sports, swimming, cycling and running - how come the sudden attraction for these forms of exercise which are on the whole natural and inherent for man?

It is certainly not a national phenomenon that has in a short time brought such an increase in the number of hobby triathletes in Germany, Europe and worldwide. Triathlon fever is booming particularly in highly industrialised countries. A possible slogan for this worldwide triathlon could be:

"Those who are clever trim their endurance forever".

The endurance sports, swimming, cycling and running, have been rediscovered as a means of combatting the much lamented lack of exercise. Triathlon sport has earned a special place among the several forms of endurance sports simply because everyone can manage swimming, cycling and running without any great previous technical knowledge, and all three of these sports offer a harmonious and natural form of exercise.

As well as meriting triathlon from a triple fitness aspect, swimming cycling and running can quite simply be fun in just the way that it is a pleasure for children to swim, to ride a bike, to run and to play. All three disciplines are in the open air and thus enable a rediscovery of nature. Swimming through a lake, cycling though fields and forests, and running through meadows and woods can be quite an experience. Probably more pleasant than the organized adventure trip by jet with a well-filled wallet. Sun, wind and weather are almost strangers nowadays to our bodies so used to central heating. Exercise outdoors can wash away a bad mood with a sudden heavy shower.

In our leisure society sport for the active members is becoming more and more important as a regulating and activating factor for body and soul. Endurance sport affects our psyche, our social behaviour but also our fitness and state of health. The training necessary for a stabilization of health (basic endurance) is much more extensive than the training specifically for competition for those enthusiastic competitive athletes. Numerous studies from the sports medicine area confirm that the gentle endurance gymnastic exercises, and the strengthening exercises in regeneration, serve to prevent vascular disease, keep us young, build up our body's immune system and reduce stress.

As well as this, triathlon is a sport for everybody. The fact that certain pre-requirements are also vital for triathlon e.g that the body is well supplied with minerals, vitamins, trace elements, carbohydrates, fatty acids and proteins clearly shows the important role nutrition plays for active triathletes.

The almost compulsory slowdown in physical movement in the past decades has its consequences, seen today in the form of numerous diseases caused by civilization. An extraordinary amount of illnesses are directly or indirectly influenced by lack of exercise. Fact is that the risk of having a heart attack is ten times higher where there is a lack of exercise combined with overweight and high blood pressure. Endurance sports counteract these and other civilization diseases in an exceptional way. Swimming, cycling and running have a privileged place here. They bring about a number of positive factors which I can only describe here in point form.

!

- A strong heart muscle, which is then able to beat more slowly at a calmer pace.
- The entire circulation is more able for regeneration and adjustment.
- Blood pressure goes back to normal through regular endurance sport.
- An increase in the lungs' oxygen intake and in the hemoglobin rate.
- A good oxygen supply , an improved metabolism and a larger energy consumption.
- Strong, well-functioning muscles and a better body control.
- A rise in the number of human 'power stations' (mitochondria) in cells, and thus an improvement in performance capacity.
- According to Dr. Aaken people with stamina are nine times less likely to develop cancer.
- Cuts down inner tension, fear and depressive moods, thus preventing the appearance of stress symptoms.

Compared with such a number of advantages of endurance training there are only a few disadvantages. These include overuse injuries and overtraining which, through a sensible organization of training, including flexibility and stretching exercises, can be almost fully ruled out. More details of this in the following chapters.

What is endurance?

Endurance is the ability to keep up a physical performance as long as possible. According to load duration we differentiate between

Type of endurance	Duration	Energy sources used up
Speed-strength load	up to 45 sec	phosphates rich in energy
Short-term endurance	45 sec-2 min	carbohydrates
Medium-time endurance	2-10 min.	mainly carbohydrates
Long-term endurance	10-60 min	partly carbohydrates, partly fats
Extreme endurance	longer than 60 min	mainly fats

The performance capacity in endurance training depends essentially on physical abilities, endurance, strength, speed and co-ordination. Performance capacity in endurance training is divided into aerobic and anaerobic areas according to energy production.

Aerobic endurance
With endurance training of medium intensity the athlete's supply of oxygen is sufficient. Performance is achieved by means of an oxygen-burning energy production. Aerobic endurance is measured through the lactate concentration in the blood. If this value lies under 2 mmol/l, the load is described as aerobic. The far-reaching, extensive positive effects of endurance sports come to fruition mostly with aerobic training.

Anaerobic training
With higher intensities the oxygen demand is greater than the oxygen supply. Sportive performance is reached here by energy production without oxygen. The lactate concentration lies above 6 mmol/l.

Endurance training normally involves a metabolism mix with either a more aerobic or more anaerobic energy production process.

3 What Is Triathlon?

"Triathlon" (Greek) - a multiple event of swimming, cycling and running - the description in a dictionary. This multiple event is a non-stop endurance event where the stopwatch is set off at the swimming startpoint and isn't stopped before the triathlete has passed the line at the running finish. Any person enjoying good health will say" I've been able to run since I was one, can cycle since pre-school and can swim since my time at school. That would mean, I'm perfectly able to start triathlon." And that's the truth. Nearly every person is able to take part in a triahlon competition.

This pleasant piece of news does not necessarily apply for the spectacular scenes, so effective for the media, for the Ironman Distance (226 km altogether) in Hawaii, Roth, Zürich, Kulmbach, Lanzarote, Canada, Australia, New Zealand, Japan or wherever, but rather for the shorter distances.

In order to make triathlon sport appealing as a popular sport, because of the variety of positive effects on one's health, the original Ironman or Hawaii Distance of 3.86 km swimming, 180.2 km cycling and 42.195 km running is halved, quartered and so on - i.e. drastically shortened..

In the meantime triathlon sport has settled on the following distances:

Event title	Swimming distance (km)	Cycling distance (km)	Running distance (km)
Children's-or mini- triathlon	0.1 – 0.4	2.5 – 10	0.4 – 2.5
Everyman's sprint triathlon	0.5 – 0.75	20	5
Olympic or short triathlon	1 – 1.5	40	10
Middle triathlon	2	80	20
Ultra triathlon (Ironman-Distance)	3.86	180.2	42.195
Double Ironman-Distance	7.92	360.4	84.4

In addition to the above there are various events where the distances differ considerably. In many cases the distances are adapted according to the local or rural conditions. Men and women of all performance levels can today choose their own competition. The only restrictions on distance are those for school children and youths in compliance with the rules of the DTU - the German Triathlon Union.

According to these the 10-11 year-old "C" colts may only compete over a maximum distance of 0.1/2.5/0.4 km, the 11-12 year-old "B" colts over 0.2/5/1 km, the 13-14 year-old "A" colts over 0.4/10/2.5 km, the 15-16 year-old youths over a maximum of 0.75/ 20/ 5 km, the same applies for the "B" juniors, the 18-19 year-old "A" juniors can compete at Olympic Distance. From then on participation in the middle-, long- or ultra-distances are also allowed.

If we want to find out whose idea it was to bring three complete endurance disciplines together to become a sport of its own, we need to go back to the year 1977. In Honolulu, Hawaii a group of members of the Waikiki-Swimming Club were sitting having a drink, discussing the three most important sport events on the island of Ohahu (whose capital is Honolulu). The "Waikiki Rough Water Swim" - a swimming competition in the Pacific Ocean covering a distance of 2.4 miles =3.86 km, the "Around Ohahu Bicycle Race" a cycling race with a distance of 112 miles =180.2 km around the island of Ohahu, and the "Honolulu Marathon" covering the known distance of 26 miles =42.195 km.
Of these three outstanding sports events which is the most difficult, and which athlete - the swimmer, the cyclist or the runner - is the best endurance sportsman?

The marine officer JOHN COLLINS then posed the question for discussion whether or not these three sporting events could be combined to form one competition of its own. Many took this idea to be a joke but COLLINS was serious in what he meant. On the 18th February 1978 15 men turned up for a competition for the first time, a competition which became worldwide, the challenge of all challenges in the years that followed and enabled triathlon to become an independent sport of its own. The entire story and the special fascination ragarding this annual sporting event in Hawaii is dealt with thoroughly in the book "Ironman - the Hawaii Triathlon".

The 'peak' in terms of recognition of this new form of sport was the decision to include triathlon as an Olympic sport in the year 2000. This did not cover the Hawaii distance however, but rather the Short or Olympic distance of 1.5/ 40/ 10 km.

Finished!

4 "Prime target" in a Triathlon - to Finish

The rapid development of triathlon in all distances has meant that it is almost the norm these days for the number of starting participants in established events to amount to several hundred triathetes. Even a starting field of 1 000 (one thousand!) is not infrequent. Some examples here: Roth approx. 2 700, Nice approx. 1 700, Hawaii approx. 1 500, Krefeld approx. 1 300.

Several million athletes worldwide take part in triathlon events; in Germany alone there are an estimated 300 000 active triathletes. In this sport there come together young and old, women and men, beginners, advanced, fitness athletes, competitive athletes, world class athletes. In which other sport has that been heard of?

The aim in the numerous team sports, athletic disciplines and indeed most other forms of sport is always to win. The mere number of participating athletes renders this clear goal orientation impossible in triathlon. If the probability of winning in a team sport involving two teams is 50%, at a tournament with three, four or five participating teams it would still be 33, 25 or 20%; for a triathlon event with 500 competitors this percentage would drop to 0.2%, in Roth with its 2 700 starters a mere 0.037%.

The great number of athletes who find triathlon competition so appealing must therefore have other reasons. The magic word here is 'finish'. To finish in triathlon means:

- You've completed it!
- You've managed it!
- You've reached your personal goal!
- You've conquered the swimming, cycling and running distances!
- You've successfully finished the competition!
- You've completed the required distances through your own muscle strength!

!

This is what so many athletes look for and find in triathlon.

Fun is a part of triathlon too

A further relevant goal for fitness athletes and competitive sportsmen is to discover one's own personal limit. As this is totally independent of the performance of the other athletes, every triathlete can participate in his own personal competition and plumb the depths of his current performance limit in the process. Awareness of the fact that one's physical performance ability is connected with one's psyche, represents a special challenge for many people of all ages. In many cases performance levels have been reached which the athlete himself would not have dreamt of. It almost goes without saying that this fact gives one's self-confidence a considerable boost.

On the other hand it is no wonder that athletes who frequently overestimate their performance ability begin to feel unsure and doubt they've completed the required distances through their own muscle strength! This is what so many athletes look for and find in triathlon. in themselves. However in order to get closer to one's genuine physical and psychic limit, an athletic development is necessary, which in triathlon sport, and in the entire area of endurance sports, takes a number of years. Short-term success does exist in triathlon sport, but it is only possible to reach one's absolute performance limit only after five to six years.

5 Why Choose Triathlon?

As well as the health aspects of triathlon sport there is a number of other reasons **WHY** individuals and an ever-increasing swarm of people of all ages succumb to the fascination of this non-stop three-event competition. Among these reasons are the following:

Triathlon keeps you fit
The all-round nature of triathlon promotes one's general fitness. Every active sportsman should become fit through endurance training. This attained level of fitness can then be put to test in competitions.

Triathlon is a "sensible" leisure-time occupation
Beginning with school pupils who have their first training sessions in swimming, cycling or running at the age of ten or eleven, then to adolescents and young adults, working men and women who, on finishing with their sprint, speed strength or team sports, now compensate these nicely through triathlon sport, up as far as the retired who still wish to stay active, one can see just what a sensible and useful leisure-time occupation triathlon is with its three forms of endurance training.

Triathlon is an everyman's sport
As already mentioned, the three forms of endurance sport swimming, cycling and running offer everyone the opportunity to take up sport. Most people have been able to swim since their childhood, the same applies for cycling, and running is a matter of pure will and training. Covering very short distances such as 200-500 m swimming, 15-20 km cycling and 2-5 km running for beginners, on to the Olympic and middle distances up as far as the long or Ironman distance, triathlon sport offers everyone a wide range of sporting activity. What counts here: you're never too old, too stiff, too tall, too small, too thin or too fat, but simply too lazy!

Triathlon competitions bring satisfaction, inner joy, contentment and an ego boost
All triathlon finishers, regardless of the distances covered, experience very pleasant feelings, often for the first time, such as joy, contentment, satisfaction and a serious boost to their ego.

Triathlon is an all-round sport and is a lot of fun

The all-round nature of triathlon can be directly attributed to the large amount of different forms of exercise possible. Apart from swimming, cycling and running, gymnastics, strength training, but also cross-country skiing and all other forms of physical training can be built in too. Furthermore, anyone who trains regularly in a group will notice that endurance sports training, with the exception of swimming, is perfect for a chat. This is needless to say not only about exchanging personal experiences in training and competitions but also about private topics. The relaxed training atmosphere promotes a further important aspect of physical activity - fun!

Triathlon is a fair form of sport and a real challenge

Triathlon is an individual sport and not a team sport like cycling for example. This clearly implies that each triathlete has to fend for himself. This is also the case for the frequent defects that a bike develops during a competition. Equality of chance is preserved to the extent that one is not allowed to accept any assistance offered, the changing of racing bikes, the use of flippers, doping, personal accompaniment for the running distances is forbidden, violation of these rules leads to disqualification.

Triathlon is an experience, it is a calculated adventure

The three fully different endurance disciplines in water, on the bike and finally on foot constitute an experience of a high order. To move forward with pure muscle strength, first by swimming, then cycling and finally running, is every time a thrilling, adventurous experience for me even after more than 120 starts. Before the start nobody can really estimate all problems and difficulties which may occur, one must simply face up to them and come to grips with them as best one can. Whoever enjoys their sport will profit more from the overall assets of triathlon. The calculated adventure of triathlon is something which even the wealthiest of this world cannot buy. The most expensive racing bike, the best shoes and a personal coach are all no guarantee of a successful triathlon. Each athlete must achieve his performance at triathlon through his own strength alone.

Triathlon offers incentives to improve oneself in several disciplines
Every triathlete, whether a fitness athlete or a competitive sportsman, gets a special kick out of improving oneself. Triathlon offers four possibilities here. As well as the three individual disciplines one can achieve further time gains through an improved swim-cycle changeover and cycle-run changeover. As triathlon is made up out of three complete forms of endurance sport, significant improvements in time can only be expected after many years of training. This demands a training programme concentrating at first on increasing training quantity, later on increasing training quality. More about this later.

Triathlon does not demand any particular athletic
pre-requirements, but does guarantee a significant growth in vitality
One of triathlon' secrets: in order to carry out triathlon successfully for oneself there are no particular physical pre-requirements, but rather only regular training, willpower and stamina. With systematic triathlon training over a longer period of time all organs, in particular heart, circulation and lungs, slowly adapt to these higher demands. Training organization will get better through the sheer pleasure derived from movement. The combination with a more sensible diet will bring about a considerable rise in vitality. Vitality, which is of benefit to everybody in his private and working life as well.

Triathlon and sensible eating go hand in hand
Just as a high-revving motor can only drive with fuel of high quality, so too should every active sportsman with performance ability supply his body with highly nutritious food. Anyone who takes this to heart without making a religion out of it, is allowed to "sin" now and again.

6 The "Triathlon Cycle" for Hobby Sportsmen

In this chapter I would like to guide all those who are new to triathlon toward their first competition. All relevant aspects will be briefly dealt with, from general fitness to the minimal equipment required, the most important training principles, the first training plans possible up as far as the competition itself. Those who wish to find out more about further levels can do so in chapter 7, which looks at the triathlon cycle for advanced or competitive sportsmen.

6.1 Triathlon - a Simple but Complex Sport

Running, swimming and cycling - as I've already mentioned most people have been able to do these things since their childhood. Are you one of these, and are you ready to find out the many advantages of triathlon for yourself? Terrific, you're almost a triathlete already.

The person who heads off and packs swimming trunks or swimsuit, has his bike in good order, ties up his running shoes to go and prove himself, will find out that apart from the three individual disciplines the following problem areas exist:

Hobby sportsmen shortly after the start

- The fourth discipline is the swim-cycle changeover.
- The fifth discipline is the cycle-run changeover.
- Quite a crowd in the water.
- Wobbly knees after swimming.
- Damp clothes while cycling.
- What drinks and food for cycling and running?
- Legs of lead in the first few kilometres of running.
- What drinks and food after the triathlon?
- How can I regenerate myself properly?

It's this variety, both in preparation and in competition, which makes triathlon sport such a complex, small - but fascinating - adventure.

The simplest and most effective way to get to reap the numerous health advantages already mentioned is to become fit through endurance training. There is no doubt at all that you too will manage this if you have the willpower. With the endurance test according to COOPER one can establish the level of personal fitness, and keep a check on the rapidly occurring improvements, in a simple way. If you have a "medium fitness" at the least, you have already managed the first and most important step towards participation in an 'Everyman's triathlon'.

6.2 General Fitness Test - Endurance Test According to COOPER

The basic prerequirement before taking up or carrying out endurance training is good health as well as knowledge about current performance ability. For this reason those persons who are over 35, or have not been physically active for a few years, should undergo a doctor's physical examination before taking up endurance training. Examinations on a treadmill and bicycle ergometer in particular have caught on in sports medicine. Of all the different fitness tests which anyone can carry out by themselves without any major difficulties, the so-called COOPER test has proved to be very worthwhile.

This running test, developed by the American sports physician and astronaut trainer Dr. med. Kenneth COOPER, can best be carried out on a 400 metre running track, as the distance run within the twelve minute running time represents one measurement of fitness. Should there be no stadium available with a suitable running track, this test can be carried out on an ordinary road. A car driving behind the runner gives the start and stop signals by horn and can read the distance covered on the tachometer.

This test involves covering the longest possible running (or running-walking) distance on a flat surface within twelve minutes and indicates the maximum current performance ability for running. The longer the distance covered in kilometres, the fitter you are. Due to the smaller muscle mass, the number of kilometres covered by women is slightly less than for men in the same fitness category.

12-minute-test (running/walking) according to COOPER

Fitness-category	Sex	13-19 yrs	20-29 yrs	30-39 yrs	40-49 yrs	50-59	60 +
I. very weak	Men	< 2.08	< 1.95	< 1.89	< 1.82	< 1.65	< 1.35
	Women	< 1.60	< 1.45	< 1.50	< 1.41	< 1.34	< 1.25
II. weak	Men	2.08-2.19	1.95-2.10	1.89-2.08	1.82-1.98	1.65-1.86	1.39-1.63
	Women	1.60-1.89	1.54-1.78	1.52-1.68	1.41-1.57	1.34-1.49	1.25-1.38
III. medium	Men	2.21-2.50	2.11-2.38	2.10-2.32	2.00-2.22	1.87-2.08	1.65-1.92
	Women	1.90-2.06	1.79-1.95	1.70-1.89	1.58-1.78	1.50-1.68	1.39-1.57
IV. good	Men	2.51-2.75	2.40-2.62	2.34-2.50	2.24-2.45	2.10-2.30	1.94-2.11
	Women	2.08-2.29	1.97-2.14	1.90-2.06	1.79-1.98	1.70-1.89	1.58-1.74
V. excellent	Men	2.77-2.98	2.64-2.82	2.51-2.70	2.46-2.64	2.32-2.53	2.13-2.48
	Women	2.30-2.42	2.16-2.32	2.08-2.22	2.00-2.14	1.90-2.08	1.76-1.89
VI. outstanding	Men	> 2.99	> 2.83	> 2.72	> 2.66	> 2.54	> 2.50
	Women	> 2.43	> 2.34	> 2.24	> 2.16	> 2.10	> 1.90

(Information in kilometres according to age)

If your fitness level lies in the first three categories i.e not so adequate, do not be discouraged, as you have this quality common with approx. 80% of civilised mankind. One should understand this result as a motive toward a well thought out training programme. This 12-minute test is not only a reliable measure of existing fitness, it also provides accurate information on running progress. As it is easy to carry out this test it enables a regular check on one's own performance ability.

Are you fit for the next stages in our triathlon cycle?

Hints and tips specifically for running come later. At this stage then, some more general statements which apply for all three endurance sports - swimming, cycling and running.

6.3 Training Principles for Hobby Sportsmen

!

- Try if possible to find a training partner or a training group in which consideration is taken to every person.
- Run and cycle at a speed at which you can still hold a conversation.
- You should always finish up training with the feeling: "I would still be able to go on swimming, cycling or running".
- Train in such a way as to still have fun.
- Training is not a competition!
- During the training session, try to organize your speed for the competition itself over a fifth or a tenth of the upcoming distance. You may then repeat this 3-5 times after an active rest interval of five minutes.
- Remember: triathlon training is endurance training!

If you have already been training according to these principles for several weeks and are about to commence the four-week preparation for a competition, we should then have a look at the minimum amount of equipment necessary.

6.4 Minimum Equipment Required for a Triathlon Competition

Every hobby sportsman, who principally goes to a swimming pool or a lake in the summer months is automatically the proud owner of suitable swimming gear. As well as the **swimming trunks** one also needs goggles and a swimming cap. With these bits and pieces you are now fully kitted out for a triathlon with summer water temperatures of about 20°.

For the second discipline, **cycling**, what is needed is a bike which works and a cycling helmet. A so-called 'road-racer' or even a typical Dutch bike might be enough on a flat surface. What's compulsory is the helmet, even at an Everyman's triathlon. At the end of the day a helmet which costs 60-80 Deutsch Marks (= approx $ 40) can, in the case of a fall, protect us from serious head injuries both in training and in competition.

The minimum **kit required for running** is really only a pair of good running shoes. However the emphasis is on GOOD. Besides the shoes, one needs a cap to protect oneself from the far too intensive sun rays in the hot summer months. All other things like a running shirt, shorts and socks are not at the top of the list at all.

So, even those of humble sportive ambition should not buy their good running shoes in the bargain basement of a department store but rather in a store specializing in these articles. Here at least you can expect good advice. This does not mean to say that the shoes are going to cost 200 Deutsch Marks (= approx. $ 100). Whoever is willing to have a little look round and is happy with a shoe from last season's collection, which is by no means inferior in quality to this season's shoes, can often end up saving 50% of the original sales price.

Why Is the Right Running Shoe so Important?
Firstly, our locomotor system is not as adaptable as our cardiovascular system, and secondly the mechanic load, even for a lightweight athlete is extraordinarily high.

A good shoe prevents overuse injuries such as:

- pes valgus
- overuse of the knee and hip joints
- hardening of the calves
- back problems
- muscular problems

and many others.

For this reason the proper running shoe must be shock-absorbent, be able to carry us forward and give support. So when buying a new pair of running shoes the following points must be taken into consideration:

!

- As most of the athlete's weight normally comes onto the heel, a running shoe needs a firm heel with good shock absorbency.
- The rim of the heel has to be soft in order to avoid achilles tendon problems.
- The upper shoe must sit well without being too tight. This is why most shoe manufacturers have shoes in different widths.
- The front of the shoe must leave enough room for the toes.
- This implies 1cm room between the shoe cap and the toes. Be aware that shoe sizes differ greatly from manufacturer to manufacturer. For example, I wear shoes from size 13 up to 14 1/2.
- In general a shoe for competition can be lighter than a training shoe since the distances run in competition are significantly shorter than all those kilometers of training.
- It's important to note whether the running shoes are mainly to be used for cross-country or road surfaces.

Furthermore, one must regard the orthopaedic aspect. One differs here between "pronation problems" and "supination problems". The group of runners with no such problems is considerably smaller than the one with problems.

Above - a light competition shoe below - compact training shoe

Many athletes are inclined to suffer from **"pronation"**. This is when the ankle bone clicks inward. One can counteract this problem with a suitable firmer shock absorbency in the inner sole area. A further number of runners are prone to **"supination"**, an outward click of the ankle bone, which can be counteracted with appropriate firmer shock absorbency in the outer sole area. Supination is a frequent result of bow legs, loose ligaments in the ankle area, or a hollow splayfoot.

Whether or not a runner is a victim of supination or pronation can be found out by having a look at his now well-worn shoes, or by means of a treadmill analysis. For this reason it is important when buying new running shoes to have the old ones with you and get some specialist advice on this. Considering the mentioned problem areas it is clear that there is no such thing as THE optimal universal shoe. For athletes this means wearing a few different models of shoe.

One can recommend here: wear at least two, but better three pairs of running shoes in rotation.

How Long Do Running Shoes Last Today?

As the durability of shoes not only depends on their age but also on the load involved, one can take the kilometres run in the shoes as a guide. The running expert Carl Jürgen DIEM estimates the 'wearability' of today's running shoes to be only 1 000 to 1 500 km. Up to 2 000 km is an exception.

6.5 Training Plans for Hobby Triathletes

Final month before an Everyman's triathlon

Day	Swimming	Cycling	Running	Remarks
Mon		30		at a moderate pace
Tue			8	
Wed		15		fast
Thu	1.0			with intervals
Fri				
Sat	0,5	15	3	**test competition**
Sun				
Total	**1.5**	**60**	**11**	

Day	Swimming	Cycling	Running	Remarks
Mon				
Tue	1.0			5 x 200 m
Wed		25		
Thu			6	at a moderate pace
Fri				
Sat		20		at a moderate pace
Sun			6	relaxed
Total	**1.0**	**45**	**12**	

Day	Swimming	Cycling	Running	Remarks
Mon	0.8			5 x 100 m
Tue		25		fast
Wed				
Thu			6	fartlek
Fri				
Sat		30		at a moderate pace
Sun	1.0		10	swim and run
Total	**1.8**	**55**	**16**	

Day	Swimming	Cycling .	Running	Remarks
Mon				
Tue			8	fast sections
Wed		25		relaxed
Thu	0.8			
Fri				
Sat	**0.5**	**20**	**5**	**Everyman's triathlon**
Sun				
Total	**1.3**	**45**	**13**	

The possible training schedule illustrated here is one of many. There are several other variations. You must find out your optimal training programme by yourself, as only you know your individual abilities.

Arrive punctually for your triathlon competition i.e. approximately 1.5 hours before the start. After collecting your starting papers go and find your changeover zone and lay it out slowly. As well as a bike, all other bits and pieces needed for cycling and running are to be placed here too. Should you need more information on this, have a look at chapter 7.4.

Apart from the changeover area, important now are the swimming, cycling and running routes. Look at these either in the locality itself or find out about them using the route plans. See it all under the motto: "Triathlon is fun."

Complete the first event swimming, calmly and without a hectic pace. You can use up your energy on the events to follow! Even if the route is partially closed off, road traffic rules must be adhered to on the cycling route. Don't take any risks - it's not worth it. Try to find your rhythm in all three disciplines as soon as possible. In the case of unexpected problems there's only one thing that helps - keep calm. In the running event in particular, look forward to the approaching finishing target. You'll manage it, you'll get there!

Finished? Congratulations - you are a real triathlete!
If you've had fun and you want to find out more, then get to grips with the triathlon cycle for the advanced and performance athletes.

7 The Triathlon Cycle for Advanced and Performance Athletes

7.1 Improved Triathlon Equipment

7.1.1 Swimming Equipment

For normal water temperatures swimming equipment consists of swimming trunks/swimsuit, a swimming cap and a pair of goggles. The goggles protect the eyes from chlorine or salt. They should be watertight and allow a wide eye radius. Goggles which are fogged up or not watertight are often a major nuisance, and one can prevent this from occurring by doing the following:

- Moisten the dry goggles on the inside with a little shampoo or saliva and then rinse out. This prevents the goggles from steaming up.
- When buying new goggles pay attention that the bridge over the nose is the correct size.
- Never wear a new pair of goggles in a competition.

!

For those athletes who wear glasses there are now special goggles with lenses. Tinted goggles make seeing easier when swimming in the open.

The complete triathlon equipment

Fashionable triathlon collection

What can you do when the water is too cold?

Athletes who are vulnerable to feeling the cold and often compete in lakes or the open sea, should really invest 500-700 DM (approx. $ 250 - 500) in a neoprene swimsuit. For shorter distances (500 - 1 000 m) a thick layer of milking grease might just do the trick to protect against the cold. However two swimming caps are definitely necessary as the majority of body heat is lost through the head.

The material of a neoprene suit may be up to 5mm thick. This suit is not only terrific for protecting from the cold, but it also improves swimming times due to the added buoyancy. There are basically two types of neoprene suits: long-leg suits with and without arms. When buying such a suit see if you still have enough room and freedom around the shoulder. If not, then you should go for a suit without arms. The suit should close relatively tightly around the neck so that water does not come between the suit and your body with every arm movement while swimming. For those very prone to cold there are neoprene caps which offer even more head protection.

For mid-summer temperatures swimming trunks and one-piece suits with extra lining in the crotch are a good idea, in particular for the shorter distances. The advantages here are that they dry off very quickly, and secondly that it is not necessary to change clothes again.

7.1.2 Cycling Equipment

Whereas the equipment for swimming and running is quite simple and conventional it starts to get a bit complicated when considering the entire cycling equipment.'Better' cycling equipment begins with 1 000 Deutsch Marks (approx. $ 500) for the racing cycle alone, and can be up to ten times the price when personal extras are requested. However the fun aspect of this varied sport does not necessarily rise in line with the cost of the equipment. One's own inner attitude is almost fully responsible for this.

Racing Cycle

Buying a racing bike is a costly and highly technical matter. Anyone who is not fully familiar with this subject must seek the advice of a specialist. It is thus advisable not only to concentrate on the price of a bike but just as much on the services offered. It's seldom that one

High-tech frame out of titanium - including fork a mere 1650 g

goes and buys a triathlon bike off the peg, but rather it is put together from a series of details by a specialized shop. Included here are: the frame, the handlebars, the front section, the gears, the brakes, the fork, the front wheel, the chain, the pedal system, pedal winders, the rear wheel, gear rims, the saddle support, the saddle, the tyres, the bottle holder, the pump, the spare tubes and the most important repair tools. For each of these points there is a large number of alternatives with great differences in price. It is of course every triathlete's goal to own a racing machine which, as well as offering a good sitting position and being light in weight, is excellent from an aerodynamic aspect, thus meeting the requirements for an optimal movement process and the best possible performance.

You can of course go and buy a racing cycle off the peg and so rid yourself of the great number of decisions. The important thing here as with all other racers is the frame height required. Anyone who makes the wrong decision on this must reckon with the fact that due to his incorrect sitting position he will not able to bring his individual capacities completely to light. Indeed he may even be risking getting injured.

The frame height is measured in centimetres, determined from the middle of the pedal bearing up to the top rim of the saddle tube. The frame height for 28 inch wheels is determined by the leg and stride length along with the approximate height of the athlete. With the 26 inch wheels, which are very popular today, a 1-2 cm lower frame height is chosen.

The following table does not give the exact frame heights, but rather offers you some help with your decisions as to the correct height.

Frame height in cm	Approx. height in m
51 – 53	1.60 – 1.65
54 – 55	1.65 – 1.70
56 – 57	1.70 – 1.75
58	1.75 – 1.80
59	1.80 – 1.85
60	1.85 – 1.90
61 – 62	> 1.90

Tailor-made frames, can only be put together by specialized constructors of frames, after taking further details such as trunk and arm length into consideration.

Handlebars and Front Section

It is impossible to imagine cycling in triathlon without the aerodynamic handlebars. Nevertheless it is still possible for every athlete to go to the start with normal racing handlebars. The gear lever is also mounted on the handlebars so that there are no difficulties changing gears in a stretched position. Depending on arm length there are different sizes for the front section.

Racing Wheels

Generally speaking all types of wheels may be used, either with 36 spokes (normal), with 16 or even only four or three. Very popular for the athletes with higher ambitions are the closed disc wheels. The advantage of these costly wheels with few spokes is simply the fact that every spoke causes an eddy. The fewer spokes there are the less air resistance generated. The resulting potential time gains depend to a large extent on the speed. An athlete who manages forty on average on his racing bike achieves considerably greater time gains with the costly wheels than someone who cycles thirty on average. The prices for front or alternatively rear wheels range from a few hundred Deutsch Marks for a normal construction up to several thousand Marks per wheel.

On a rear wheel is of course the gear rim. This consists of 6-8 individual pinions with a different number of teeth. The grading of the rims depends on the following factors:

- training state
- size of racing wheels (28 or 26 inch)
- surface/terrain for training or competition

On an even surface, and for normal training, rims with a greater number of teeth are mostly used, for competition or intensive training rims with less teeth. However it is not the amount of teeth and rims that is important, but rather the revolutions per minute.

On the chain disc at the front one normally uses 52/42 but also 53/39 teeth for 28 inch wheels. The decisive factor here is the grading of the rim at the back. For flat surfaces a grading of 13-23 teeth is enough, but for upward gradients one would need 13-26 or even 13-28. With 26 inch wheels both the chain (56/43) and the back rims are graded somewhat differently (12-21, 12-23).

When choosing tyres more and more people are turning to wire tyres these days as opposed to the tube tyres. The former has a separate tube inside which can be changed quickly when necessary. This is not the case for the tube tyres - they are glued to the wheel rim.

When deciding on the right pedals, it's important to choose a system which allows the shoes a quick clicking in and out. These advantages are not as important for a swift changeover in competition as for an easy disengagement at junctions and traffic lights when in training. The now numerous pedal systems, in combination with a good cycling shoe, also enable an optimal force transmission and 'round' pedalling. Further decisive factors in feeling comfortable on a racing bike are **a sitting position**, saddle and cycling pants.

If you're not comfortable on your racing bike you can't expect to achieve good performance. So the racing bike must become an extended part of your body. This means that the saddle must be so high as to allow me as an athlete to transmit my force from the rear wheel to the road as economically as possible. Determining the correct saddle height is something you can only manage to do after many training sessions, during which you really have to take a critical look at the sitting position. You should however pay attention to the following points to get a rough guide:

Adjustment of Saddle Height

Sit on your bike with your shoes on. One pedal is at its lowest position. The saddle is at its right height when your leg is almost outstretched and the heel of your shoe touches the pedal. Important! Don't slide down sideways from the saddle.

Correct Positioning of Saddle

Finding the right saddle position is a matter which varies from person to person. Some athletes have the saddle set to a completely horizontal position and have no problems whatsoever. Other athletes adjust the saddle to have it pointing slightly upwards towards the front section. This position certainly saves men from problems with impotence and women from uncomfortable bruising.

The important thing is that you feel comfortable on your bike.

Cycling pants with a special leather lining in the crotch prevent chafing and ensure a pleasant, comfortable sitting position particularly over long distances.

The cycling jersey and **drinks bottles** are the things that you indirectly need as far as food and drink is concerned. At a later stage in this book I deal with the importance attached to the intake of food both in training and competition. The cycling jersey has room for food which is vital particularly over the long training and competition distances (middle and long distances). Furthermore the jersey protects sensitive parts of the body from strong sunshine, as well as doubly covering the vulnerable kidney area through its snack pockets.

A bike computer and **cycling gloves** are handy things to have; the computer for checking one's performance by way of average speed, and for checking the length of distances and possibly the pedalling frequency; the gloves ensure at least some protection of the hands in the case of a fall. The item however which offers us athletes the greatest amount of safety, thus making it the most important thing of all must be briefly mentioned here: **the helmet**. With today's traffic the way it is, the helmet must be worn at all times, both in training and in competition. Weighing often a mere 250 g cycling helmets have got more and more stylish over the past few years and have now become an absolute MUST for every triathlete. The numerous air slits in the latest helmets means that air gets through to the head even at high temperatures. So, a helmet costing 80-100 DM ($ 40-50) should not be too expensive for any of us, when you consider that they are the best preventative measure there is against serious and critical head injuries. A clavicular fracture knits together again quite quickly, a serious skull injury might never do so at all!

A well-sitting pair of **cycling shades** protects the eyes from strong sunshine and from unpleasant flies. However sweat which in turn impedes your sight is a real nuisance. Having little cloths with you for wiping the glasses is just not a practical solution for a triathlete.

!

Therefore the following tip:
The most effective method of combatting this annoying problem is with a small piece of apple. Dab a freshly cut piece of apple on the glasses both inside and outside and then dry the lenses again carefully. You now have a clear view for several hours. Any drops of sweat which appear can be got rid of with a quick shake of the head.

Does a Top Bicycle Automatically Imply a Top Placement?
I definitely have to answer this question with a loud 'No'.
When kitting oneself out for triathlon most athletes have to ask themselves the simple question: How much money am I willing to spend on my hobby triathlon? If my demands are modest, then I will manage it all with a more modest bicycle too. If I set my demands very high, both from a financial and the consequent training aspect, and this all lies within my financial limits, it's perfectly easy to get a bicycle which will cost you as much as a second-hand car in good condition. But be careful, a bicycle for 10 000 Deutsch Marks is not going to cycle the triathlon for you on its own. Athletes like Thomas Hellriegel or Jürgen Zäck on a 1 000 DM ($ 500) bicycle will still be way ahead of most other triathletes, even when all of these are going around on - 'high-tech' bicycles which are ten times the price!

7.1.3 Running Outfit

In addition to the normal running shoes as basic equipment, ambitious triathletes would need to purchase more compact shoes with better shock absorbency for training and a lighter pair for competitions.

Another further relevant point for competitions at least is the use of easy-opening 'Tanka' or 'Velcro' running shoes. Triathlon clothing is otherwise optimal to the effect that the clothing one is already wearing for swimming can similarly be worn again for cycling and running without losing time through changing.

What's perfect for this is a pair of swimming trunks with extra lining in the crotch and a tight-fitting jersey or 'top'. This competition clothing can be worn under a neoprene suit.

In order to avoid any health risks, however, I would recommend wearing this particular type of clothing when temperatures outside are 18° or more.

7.1.4 What Outfit Is Required in the Winter Months?

Any athlete who can't get through the winter without his racing or mountain bike, can protect himself from the cold and the wet more effectively with several thin layers than with a few thick ones. Neoprene caps and galoshes also do their fair share in stopping the cold from getting in. One item of equipment should by no means be done without in the winter months and that is the helmet. Widen your chin straps a little thus allowing enough room for the already mentioned neoprene cap, and then have ear covering in the form of a headband. One should never underestimate the danger of falling or slipping on a mountain bike tour through the forest.

An absolute must for running, apart from multi-layered clothing, is neon strips for the dark. Better still are those light-up systems specially developed for pedestrians or joggers which can be attached to the arms or legs. Shoes with treaded soles and a torch are a further supplement to one's winter equipment.

For the first event, **swimming**, there aren't any specific items of equipment, apart from a particularly good neoprene suit including a neoprene swimming cap for very cold water temperatures. The important thing to note here is that this suit to protect you from the cold may be no thicker than 5 mm.

As well as good running shoes, which every beginner should be wearing anyway, there aren't many items of clothing to be mentioned for **running** either. One would be the triathlon one-piece suit, or alternatively swimming trunks with lining + top, another the devices for measuring pulse and lactate.

With **cycling** however there are many pieces of extra equipment which on the one hand bring time gains, on the other require high to very high funding. The upper limit is bound to be a five-figured amount. One thing though before I go on; the best financial capacities, and the resulting most expensive equipment, will not save any athlete from having to train. There simply isn't a racing bike which can cover the cycling distance on its own without much individual effort. The most expensive equipment is not always the best. Athletes who can't really be counted as lightweight (like myself for example with my 1.86 m and 78 kg) should seriously consider whether it's the right

High-tech equipment: trispoke as front wheel, disc as rear wheel

thing to always have the lightest racing wheels, the lightest saddle support, the lightest tyres, the lightest bicycle parts. Most of these particularly light bicycle parts are also the expensive ones. When these specially light elements are the cause of certain defects in competition that's no help to anyone. As triathletes and the industry around it have by now become more inventive and innovative, it's not just a good functionability which makes a triathlete's appearance, it's often the visual effects which are the decisive factor in certain

Even the most expensive bike is safe in the bike shuttle

cases. I do not wish to conceal the psychological advantages of ultra modern cycling equipment.

All parts of a triathlon bicycle can however be purchased in simple, medium or high quality. My advice here: beginners should start out with a simple to medium quality. Should the demands be higher after some time then one can quickly and easily purchase a new, more expensive triathlon bicycle from a specialist shop while still using the old one for training. The exclusive bicycle is only to be used for intensive training sessions (speed training) and competitions.

High-quality racing machines should only be bought in specialist shops as the maintenance of the bicycle is an extremely relevant factor for good functioning.

Let's get to the point here: what athletes find it worthwhile investing in equipment which can cost up to 10 000 Deutsch Marks (app. $ 5 000)? Athletes who are able to cycle with sponsored materials. Performance-oriented sportsmen, but also beginners, who simply enjoy their terrific bicycle, can afford it and are more motivated in training because of this special love. These athletes get their kick from e.g. their soft-ride frame, their Habo-disc, their Zipp- front wheel, or their spinergy 4-spoke racing wheel, their Campagnolo gears, their

Speedplay titanium pedal, their Carnac cycling shoes, their Jet Stream drinking system, their Controltech- quick-tightener, their Syntace handlebars, their PBC pedal crank, their Titec saddle support etc. Athletes who are on the verge of entering international class and who may be able to reap significant financial advantages through their sport.

Triathletes who are able to manage 40 km per hour on average. This group of athletes benefit from the technical specialities, e.g. a larger disc than for those who cycle 30 km per hour on average

7.2 Training Principles for Advanced Athletes

!

- After an active regeneration period of a few months e.g. October-December/January in which you only have relaxed, easy-going training, then begin again with gentle running and technique training for swimming.
- The months February, March and April are perfect for specific training blocks i.e. training for one event intensively while neglecting the other two.
- An athlete must be 'well-prepared' for training holidays. This specifically means: never head off to a springtime training camp in Mallorca, Tuscany region or wherever where 100 km cycling is on the agenda every day when your own legs have only managed a total of 300 km up to this meeting.
- It's important to check your resting pulse rate during these training holidays. If your rate is 5-10 beats per minute higher than usual then only regenerative training should be done.
- Pay particular attention to diet in these intensive training phases. A lot of protein, little fat, carbohydrates come automatically.
- Hear the signs your body gives you and rectify any oncoming problems in time.
- Carry out changeover training once a week in the month of May.
- Gradually increase training load over a period of two or three weeks, only to reduce it drastically again for one week. So that makes three 'load' weeks: one relieving week, but 2:1 and1:1 are also possible. Similarly it's also possible to have this ratio 1:1, 2:1 or 3:1 for load days and relieving days.

- When increasing training, raise training frequency first, then training volume and finally training intensity.
- Never neglect basic endurance.
- Never organize training strictly but rather make it variable.
- Check training intensity with pulse measurement device.
- Train regularly.
- Performance oriented training implies giving priority to one's weakest event.
- Never train for all you're worth; it should always be fun.
- Organize swimming training with a lot of interval training for variety.
- Have other athletes observe and correct your swimming style. Organize cycling training to have approx.100 revolutions per minute. With the exception of speed training the average speed on a bicycle should lie well under competition speed.
- Don't train most of the time with aerodynamic handlebar position.
- For your own safety never cycle without a helmet.
- Constantly have food and drinks with you on the bicycle in order to keep blood sugar levels in order.
- Always make sure to have good shoes for running.
- When at all possible carry out long endurance and intensive running sessions in a group.
- Consciously reduce training drastically both in volume and intensity on the last days before a competition.
- An athlete who wants to take part in competitions should in the final two months be training double the distances of the upcoming competition per week.
- Never see training plans as a dogma. Always take account of one's personal overall load.
- The longer the training unit, the less intensive the training must be.
- However tall the ambitions in sport may be, we must never forget that sport serves to promote our health and never the other way around!
- Don't turn every training session into a competition.
- Always arrive in good time to competitions.
- Before a competition only eat foods which are easy to digest.
- In competition only cycle with parts that are tried, tested and reliable. The same holds for food taken during competition.

Training correctly is an art with growing degrees of difficulty, from the beginner to the competitive athletes up as far as top-level athletes. A performance-oriented athlete who trains without any structure whatsoever in his training may well have a lot of fun with his sporting action but will not reach his declared goal. Training planning does not only revolve around load aspects such as training volume and intensity, but also takes into account individual fcators such as age, previous performance development, mental strength, willpower, sport capacities, as well as private and occupational stress factors - in other words the triathlete's entire environment. Exact and detailed instructions for training can be found in the book "The Complete Guide to Triathlon Training" and are only looked at briefly here.

Particular features for high performance triathletes
Triathletes who complement their working lives with 15, 20 or even 25 hours training a week are not necessarily satisfied with merely reaching the finishing line. This, understandingly enough, is particularly true for those professional training athletes who even train for 30 or 40 hours week in week out.
For this group of athletes it's not only a well-thought out training programme (determined by performance checks among other factors) that counts, but rather particularly the specific triathlon equipment, the so-called high-tech equipment which plays an important role.

7.2.1 Performance Checking as a Means of Training Control

An athlete who trains to compete wishes to improve his sport performance. The basis of an effective training programme lies in the fact that the human body will only give an optimal reaction to training stimulus within a specific pulse rate range. Anyone who exceeds this range for a longer period can do damage to his body. Anyone who doesn't even reach the minimum pulse rate needed isn't doing anything to improve his fitness and his strived for improvement in performance. The upper and lower range depends on the individual training state and age, and training should be carried between these two bands. The starting point for all ways of looking at training control and performance checks is a pulse measurement. Pulse can be measured with two or three fingers on the inside of the wrist down

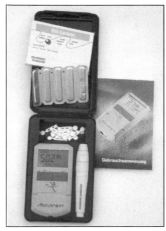

Lactate measuring device Accusport by Hestia

Pro-trainerX-C (349 DM) mit tachometer (59 DM) by POLAR, an ideal running and cycling partner

from the thumb bone, on the throat or alternatively with the aid of pulse monitors. The most accurate rates are given by the so-called 'pulsecoach' e.g. a pulse measurement device by POLAR. Training should take place within the upper and lower range, and this range is for a normal trained athlete between 120 and 150 pulse beats per minute. In order to retain a particular pulse rate throughout training, a pulse monitor is suitable for constant, regular checking. With this gadget as a training partner every athlete is able to keep an eye on his heart rate. For this purpose a special sensor belt is fastened around the thorax, which transmits the heart beats to the pulse receiver at the wrist or on the handlebars when cycling. With some of these pulse monitors it is possible to get the full pulse curve from training, or a competition printed out on a computer.

Resting pulse rate

On top of this it's important for performance-oriented triathletes to know the resting pulse rate or resting heart rate. You should take this measurement early morning before you get up i.e. lying down. Adults out of training would have a resting pulse rate of 65-80. Competitive athletes in endurance events have rates of about 50 beats per minute.

Top-level athletes are known to have pulse rates of 40 and less. Measuring resting pulse rates is highly important in two respects.

- A slow and even pulse in spring is a sign of an improved training state.
- A rate with 8-10 beats more than usual per minute indicates health problems. This is either a sign of over-training or the first signs of an oncoming 'flu infection. The risk of overtraining is particularly high during or after training camps.
- With an accelerated pulse rate you should reduce training volume and intensity immediately and only do regeneration training.

Maximal pulse

As the maximal pulse (maximal heart rate) is the basis for all pulse-related training sessions, all performance-oriented athletes should know this rate and update it every 3-4 weeks.

How do I find out my maximal pulse?

It's possible to get this rate e.g. from 3 000 km on the treadmill or a tempo run over 2 000 m in a small group, starting off in both cases of course with a warm-up run of 20 minutes. The highest pulse rate reached during this exercise indicates the maximal heart rate for running. This statistic depends first and foremost on the training state and the athlete's age. The following formula gives a rough guide: Maximal pulse = 220 - age.

7.2.2 The Four Regions of Pulse Rates According to Differing Training Loads

An athlete beginning with competitive training must obviously train in different regions to the already competitive athletes. While the first two regions are particularly important for beginners, regions 3 and 4 constitute the main share of training for advanced and performance-oriented athletes.

1. Health region with a pulse of approx. 50-60% of the maximal heart rate

All training beginners, or athletes after an inactive phase, should train with this pulse. Training is relaxed and easy and still has many positive health effects to offer.

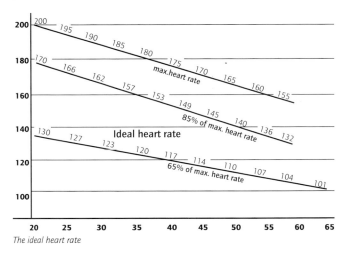

The ideal heart rate

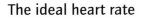

Heartbeats per minute

The ideal heart rate

2. Fat-burning region with a pulse of approx. 60-70% of
maximum heart rate

With this load the body gets the chance to bring in fats as the main supplier of energy. This is the case when load duration is for an hour or more. The training intensity is not high enough for the lactate formed to prevent the burning of fat. This region depicts the regenerative training for performance-oriented athletes.

3. Aerobic region with a pulse of approx. 70-80% of the
maximum heart rate

This level in training is the one in which triathletes move most from the point of view of time. This is the standard training region. Training here is perceived to be 'medium load' or even 'exertion'. If you want to improve your performance, i.e. become quicker in running, cycling or swimming, then this region is particularly important for you. Energy for movement is released by the fats and carbohydrates. The more intensive the load, the more carbohydrates are needed to supply energy.

4. Anaerobic region with a pulse of approx. 80-100% of the
   maximal heart rate

You should only train at this level if you wish to improve your anaerobic capacity. It is for performance-oriented athletes. Training at this level is perceived to be 'hard-going' or 'very exertive'. Prerequirement for this type of training is a very well developed aerobic basic endurance.

7.2.3 Taking Your Pulse - Different Aspects Depending on Type of Sport

The pulse rates while running are generally the fastest. As the organic load through cycling and swimming is less than for running, the corresponding pulse rates are also slower. The pulse rate for running is 5-10 beats faster per minute than for cycling and 10-15 beats faster than for swimming. In other words:

Cycling pulse   = Running pulse - 5 to 10 beats per min.
Swimming pulse   = Running pulse - 10 to 15 beats per min.

7.2.4 Lactate Measurement

When we talk about lactate measurement we mean the concentration of salt in the blood's lactic acid. Lactate forms when muscles are being put to work without a sufficient oxygen supply i.e. in particular with anaerobic metabolism. Triathletes and other endurance sportsmen do not welcome lactate formation as it hinders muscle effort thus affecting one's sport performance. With the aid of lactate and pulse measuring instruments it is possible to select the training levels as well as keep a check of the training intensities carried out. According to HOTTENROTT one can assume the following connections between the maximal pulse rate for running and the corresponding lactate values:

% of maximum pulse when running	lactate rate in mmol/l	form of training
	ca. 1.0	normal everyday movement
60 – 70%	< 1.50	regeneration training
70 – 80%	< 2.0	aerobic training (basic endurance training)
80 – 90%	2-6	aerobic-anaerobic training (endurance training)
90 – 100%	> 6	anaerobic training (interval training)

How often the one or the other training form comes to be used within a week of training depends on your state of performance, the performance capacities, and the training phase you are currently in.

In general the rule is for endurance athletes: The longer the unit of training the slower the training speed.

How and when should lactate be measured?

Lactate is measured at different degrees of load in all three of the endurance sports, swimming, cycling and running. The distance for running should be 2 000 m which is to be covered 4-6 times. Begin with a speed at which you can comfortably move at the aerobic level. Then the lactate and incurring pulse rates are measured. For this purpose the company HESTIA has developed the so-called lactate quick-measuring device "Accusport" for a price of around 600 Deutsch Marks ($ 300). Following this procedure, with every further 2 000 m run the speed is increased up as far as total capacity.

Suitable distances for cycling are 6 km done 4-6 times, and for swimming 400 m covered 4-6 times. The relation between pulse rates and these lactate measurements can be shown graphically and be used for the remaining training effort.

7.2.5 Triathlon and the Ozone

Our sports activity revolves around nature and this means for us triathletes that we begin to develop a particular awareness of the environment. Thus it is necessary for us to appropriately put this knowledge of the environment into practice. This includes making an active effort towards a reduction of the ozone hole in the stratosphere. The physicist Carl-Jürgen DIEM says in his book "Tips for Success - Running for Beginners" that there is no evidence, either general or from the area of sports science, to show that the heavily discussed ozone level of 200 mg/cbm is damaging for mankind. A drop in performance of 10% has only been accounted for at ozone levels of 600 mg/cbm. In areas of the United States there are areas where ozone levels of 1 000 mg/cbm have been measured and no damage to performance is known of.

Triathlon even with high ozone levels?

As high ozone levels come together with very high temperatures and high air humidity, it is the last two factors which can cause problems. The following measures can be recommended with this in mind:

- Reduce training intensity,checking it with the aid of pulse measuring instruments.
- Give priority to cycling and swimming rather than running.
- Carry out training early in the mornings or late in the evenings.

7.2.6 Triathlon in the Heat

Who doesn't wish for nice weather for triathlon? However, nice weather can also mean high temperatures and sultriness. You should then pay attention to the points above for training, a few more points are relevant for competition:

- Begin with drinking very early on.
- Drink plenty before, during and after the competition.
- Wear bright clothing and suncap.
- At the first signs of overheating cut down on load immediately and make sure that even more fluid is taken.
- Use sun protection cream repeatedly for competition and long training phases.

A few comments about clothing. There really is a noticeable difference in temperature between bright and dark materials. This is why it is imperative for athletes with thick, dark or even sparse hair to wear a white cap. The cycling cap has proven itself in this respect because as well as offering sun protection it offers you the chance to throw a capful of water over yourself while running. Since about a third of body cooling takes place in the head and throat areas you should be careful about using a headband. It may prevent the sweat from pouring onto your face but it can cause heat congestion.

While running it's a good idea to to have a little plastic tube with you. This makes drinking easier and enables you to finish the beaker.

7.2.7 Triathlon in the Cold

The already mentioned DTU (German Triathlon Union) has several regulations for when the water temperatures are too low. Depending on how low the temperature is in the water it may be necessary to shorten the swimming distances. On top of this the following measures are advisable:

● Wear a neoprene suit and cap.
● Change your clothing after each event.
● Wear clothes which will keep you warm, and also perhaps clothing which will protect you from the rain, even if this means losing a good few seconds on your time. It's better to just accept these few minutes than to put your health at risk!

!

For training in autumn and winter the so-called nordic underwear can be recommended e.g. by Odlo. This underwear transports the body's moisture to the layer on top (e.g. T-shirt) thus keeping the body nice and warm.

7.2.8 Triathlon and Sex

This theme can often build up into a real problem for some strict, performance-oriented athletes who are preparing optimally for a triathlon competition. The fact that sex was involved before the actual sport challenge itself - will this impair my sport performance in the competition?

For well-trained endurance athletes who before a competition wish to follow their natural sexual drive with ther partner and then go into competition feeling free and elated this can by no means be a disadvantage. An athlete who after pre-competition sex feels mentally strained, or is already able to find a reason for his failure later, would be better to do without. A simple tip here for every athlete and his private life, we have to learn through experience. Who can stop us?

7.3 Training Plans for the Olympic Distance

The basis, and simultaneously the main component, for performance for **all** types of endurance sport with competitions lasting from a few minutes to several hours is, was and always will be **basic endurance training.** It is also known as aerobic training and lays the foundation for high competition speeds; this must take place all year round being particularly intensive in the preparation phases.

The greater the endurance performance capacity, the quicker one can run, cycle and swim under aerobic metabolism conditions.

The most common mistake made by triathletes is to select a training intensity at this very important level which is simply too high. This is the cause of medium- to long-term states of overtraining. I see this happening often particularly with young athletes, and also in the so-called spring training camps. Iron discipline, common sense and the knowledge that individual highest performances in all types of endurance sport are only possible after at least five or six years are the most important pre-requirements. Whoever is active in endurance sport does not only need staying power but a lot of patience too. These statements seem somewhat irrational for athletes on account of the fact that competition loads take place at considerably higher levels of intensity. Training within endurance performance capacity leads to characteristic changes in the organism, which are in turn responsible for developments in performance. In this way the number and size of the mitochondria, our own little power stations, grows. At the same time a change in enzyme activity comes about - enzymes have a part to play taking in and making use of oxygen while fats and carbohydrates are burnt. This entire adapting process takes place so slowly that the first improvement in performance can only be seen after about a month.Training within endurance performance capacity i.e.with oxygen in balance, leads to the new formation of and improved functioning of the mitochondria. Training within the aerobic-anaerobic endurance capacity enhances principally the oxygen intake of the mitochondria.

A triathlete's training underpins a wide range of possibilities for sport activities. This includes:

a) Sportsmen who wish to take part in an Olympic Distance triathlon and have over the last few weeks before the contest been doing swimming 2x weekly, running 2x and cycling 2x a week, or alternatively swimming 1x per week, running 3x (running is their strongest discipline) and cycling 2x weekly.

b) Performance-oriented athletes who in preparation for the Ironman do swimming 3x a week, cycling 4x a week, and running 3x a week.

c) High performance athletes who not only strive for a victory in their age category but furthermore a completing time of 8.45 hours for the Ironman Distance; for this goal invest up to 14 hours of training a week.

The frequency range of training for advanced or performance-oriented athletes can vary (and be enough) from an investment of 6 hours' training up to 30 or even 40 hours' training per week.

For this large group of triathletes, the very important aspects such as the build-up for a year and the entire triathlon concept are dealt with in detail in the book "The Complete Guide to Triathlon Training" and for this reason will not be repeated here.

This is also why I've only drawn up a training guide for the Olympic Distance in this book. This should indicate how you can train - can and not must - to reach the goal you have set for yourself. With all these suggestions please always pay attention to the important tips and basic principles for swimming, cycling and running from chapter 7.2.

Four weeks for advanced and performance oriented athletes

Day	Swimming	Cycling	Running	Remarks
Mon				rest day
Tue	2.0			4x100 m + 4x200 m
Wed		50	12	
Thu		35		intervals
Fri			15	easy
Sat	2.5			
Sun		60	10	cycling+running
total	4.5	145	37	

Day	Swimming	Cycling	Running	Remarks
Mon				regeneration week
Tue	2.0	30		calm
Wed			8	
Thu		50		easy
Fri	2.5			short intervals
Sat			15	calm
Sun		40		
total	4.5	120	23	

Day	Swimming	Cycling	Running	Remarks
Mon	2.0			1,2,3,4,5,4,3,2,1 B.
Tue		60	8	cycling + running
Wed		50		calm
Thu	1.5			
Fri			15	5x1000 m speed
Sat		70		100 rpm
Sun	2.5		12	pyramid swimming
total	6.0	180	35	

Day	Swimming	Cycling	Running	Remarks
Mon	1.5			intervals
Tue			15	5.000 m fast
Wed	2.0			easy
Thu		30		calm
Fri				
Sat	**1.5**	**40**	**10**	**Olympic Triathlon**
Sun		30		very calm
total	**5.0**	**100**	**25**	

Finally one more piece of advice: the possible training schedule illustrated here is one of many. You must find out the optimal amount of training for yourself as only you know your individual abilities. An experienced coach can be of help. Triathletes with ambitions to win are often well able to do two or three times the amount of training illustrated above.

7.4 Organisation Behind a Triathlon Competition

The organisation necessary in preparation of a triathlon competition can be compared with hardly any other sport. Anyone who presumes it to be just as easy as for a 10 km run will soon notice that there is a series of further aspects to be considered. But it's exactly this preparation of one's own contest down to the final detail which makes triathlon so interesting and exciting. A very early registration is necessary for many of the big triathlon events. It must often be in several months beforehand. Even for the smaller events there is often a run for entry places. For this reason you should enter yourself for a competition as early as possible. After sending off their application as requested every starter normally gets a confirmation of registration. In the competition description forms one can find information as to the length of each individual distance, the starting time, the degree of difficulty in the different phases, and all details you need to know relating to the competition. Here are the most important points which if not adhered to can lead to a disqualification.

- Cycling only with a helmet.
- For cycling wear the starting number on your back.
- Obey road traffic rules as the roads are normally not closed off.
- For running wear the starting number on the front.
- Outside help or looking after is forbidden.
- One must wear a top of some form for running and cycling events.
- Slipstream cycling is forbidden.

On the day before the competition pack the following pieces of equipment and clothing. Certain items of equipment are needed according to type of weather and competitive distance.

Before the competition you require:
- Starting documents
- Light, easy to digest food three hours before start.

For swimming you require:
- Swimming trunks/swimsuit, cap
- Perhaps neoprene suit and vaseline
- Goggles, ear plugs, perhaps towel

For cycling you require:
- Racing cycle equipped with pump, two spare tubes, full drinks bottles
- Energy bar with adhesive strip which can be then attached to the frame.
- Helmet, shades, cycling shoes, perhaps cycling shorts, top or cycling jersey.
- Elastic band with attached starting number, perhaps cycling gloves.

For running you require:
- Quick-opening worn in shoes
- Perhaps a running top with starting number at the front, otherwise turn the number on elastic band to the front.
- Light running shorts and cap.

After the competition you require:
- Dry clothing, comfortable shoes, massage oil or 'Kanne's Brottrunk' to rub on the legs, shower gear, hand towel
- Food and drink which compensate for the loss of water, minerals and energy.

When going about the organization for a triathlon competition long before the event itself, one begins with the question: which competition am I going to take part in in the first place.

Only a well organised changeover zone enables fast changes

7.5 Laying Out of the Changeover Zone

It's getting serious now! Shortly before the start of a competition not only beginners but also experienced triathletes sometimes ask themselves: "Why am I doing this to myself today? ", or "Is this really necessary today?".

These oncoming doubts are actually a sign of the right attitude. Of course 'this' isn't necessary today. Of course every athlete can live without this thrill of a triathlon competition, but...... This 'but' is what makes triathlon so fascinating.

The nervous tension before a competition is o.k. But as soon as you hear the starting signal all these doubts are gone in a second. So let's have a long, careful look at the laying out of the changeover zone. An hour before the competition begins you should think of and consider the following:

Let us assume that both changeovers are at the same place.

The racing cycle must be secured on a stand. Place the helmet and shades on the handlebars. Fill both bottles (for short distances one bottle is often enough), close them properly and place them in the holders. The spare tubes and pump are a fixed part of equipment and should be on the bike at all times. Check that you have both tyre removers.

For 26 inch wheels you must have 26 inch tubes! If an athlete has both 28 inch and 26 inch pieces of equipment it can cause mix-ups which can be extremely annoying when you notice this during a defect in the middle of a triathlon competition. I too have had the misfortune of this experience once in a duathlon.

Cycling shoes should either be clicked into the pedals or laid beside the bike.

Whether or not socks are worn in competition is a question of habit. Every triathlete over short triathlon distances should try even in training to do without socks. Performance-oriented athletes go without socks most of the time thus saving precious moments in the changeover zone. With a cycling distance of 180 km this is possibly a different matter. Who already has soreness, chafing and bruising after 100 km would then give anything for a pair of socks.

The same is true for cycling shorts. I can only recommend these for the longer distances. A distance of 40 km on a bicycles, as in the Olympic Triathlon, is perfectly manageable in a pair of swimming trunks with suitable lining in the crotch. Some athletes even manage 180 km in swimming trunks.

If a cycling jersey is needed then it should be lying on top of or beside the bicycle. In warm weather it is normal to be wearing the top under the neoprene suit. One can sort out the matter of the starting number in the same way. If you don't use a neoprene suit for swimming then the start number and the top or the jersey must be there at hand beside your bike. All the different items of clothing can be laid out on a towel, and this you can use to dry yourself off a little.

What has proved to be very handy in the changeover zone is a fold-up plastic box where you can put your neoprene suit after taking it off. Another thing: seeing that your neoprene suit costs several hundred DM you should have your name on it. A waterproof pen is particularly suitable for this purpose. On return from the cycling distance, your running shoes and, if the weather's warm, a cap should be at hand, and perhaps light running top or shorts if necessary.

Place all these items clearly and tidily in the order in which you need them, either beside or behind each other. Athletes with not much practice should get to grips with the necessary changes in training.

If the swim-cycle and cycle-run changeovers are not in the one place then everything is spread out somewhat, and you have to be even more sure to place all pieces of equipment exactly at the right place.

For cooler weather you should place a windcheater or an extra T-shirt in the changeover zone. You will still have enough time during the competition to decide what you need and what not.

7.6 Swimming

In this fifteen point listing of the triathlon cycle we are not looking at swimming here from the training aspect, this is described in detail in the book "The Complete Guide toTriathlon Training", but rather at the essential features of swimming during a competition. These are summarised with tips to help you to successfully get through this first discipline, which for many triathletes is the most difficult discipline of all.

7.6.1 Peculiarities of Triathlon Swimming

Swimming in triathlon differs in a number of ways from swimming as an individual sport.

> Triathlon swimming competitions take place
> - mostly in open waters and thus without exact orientation
> - at lower temperatures than in a swimming pool
> - with waves
> - first before the other two endurance sports
> - often in salt water
> - in large groups.

The use of a neoprene suit is another characteristic. Whereas the first points make triathlon swimming more difficult than swimming as an individual sport, the neoprene suit makes swimming in open waters easier with its improved buoyancy.

However as regards the swimming technique there are no major significant differences between the two sports. These would be the reduced leg work on the long distances, and the fact that rhythm and breathing have to adapt to the frequent changing conditions.

This reduced swimming effort in a triathlon competition can be attributed firstly to the fact that the legs are heavily in demand in the following two endurance sports, and secondly the neoprene suit gives you a better position in the water.

Athletes who train only in a swimming pool must mentally get to grips beforehand with the following more significant differences, and furthermore they must try swimming in open waters in the summer months in order to get a bit used to some incalculable factors at least.

The significant differences are as follows:

The ever-changing wave swell and the different currents can make it necessary to adapt swimming rhythm and breathing according to the change in conditions. This implies in effect a change from three to two strokes which does of course have an effect on one's swimming style, but due to the external conditions is vital for the swimmer.

There are also big differences between the two events from a tactical point of view. In triathlon there are fundamentally no individual starts. With the normal group or mass starts, whether one runs into the water

Before the swimming start

Shortly after the swimming start

First phase finish-swimming

or starts directly in the water,- one always has to reckon with the many other competitors. Because of these unavoidable obstacles it is much more difficult to find one's own proper swimming style and swimming speed. You can avoid this problem either by heading for the outer edge of the competitive field, or, if you're a very good swimmer you can get ahead of the others with a sprint start.

A further problem in triathlon swimming in open waters is keeping the right direction. In a normal swimming pool this is ensured by the black lines so that one doesn't keep looking forward as a means of orientation, but this looking ahead is absolutely vital outside. It's a good idea to look in front to a fixed target every ten strokes. What use is it for a good swimmer when he swims a few hundred metres extra because of loss of orientation? Don't rely on the swimmer in front of you, he too may swim off line.

What problems can occur through swimming in unfamiliar saltwater? Here are two important tips: firstly a seaside holiday a few months before can get you accustomed enough to the salt, and secondly do not take milk or any dairy products directly before going into the saltwater. This causes nausea with a number of athletes.

As two further endurance events come after swimming, it is not worth giving your all for the final 300 m and thus going into oxygen debt. A pure swimmer can afford the corresponding hyperacidity of the muscles as his competition is ended after the swim. For a triathlete it only really begins after the swim. An athlete who comes out of the water having gained maybe 20 seconds but in oxygen debt will definitely lose 1-2 minutes in the necessary regeneration on the bicycle in the first phase. It's better to reduce your speed for the last 200 m of swimming which gives you the chance of a quick swim-cycle changeover.

7.6.2 Tips for Swimming Training and for Competition

- Front crawl swimming is the fastest.
- In open water orientation guides in the background are important (towers, trees)
- Try to find your swimming rhythm as soon as possible.
- Concentrate on your own technique.
- Coming up to a competition swim now and again - not all the time- in a neoprene suit.
- During training do a lot of interval swimming with short breaks. An athlete who always swims at one speed will never get faster.
- Organize your swim session in such a way that it has variety.
- Also train regularly in a group.
- Remember: the risk of injury through overuse of the joints, ligaments and tendons is much lower in swimming than in any other endurance sport.

7.6.3 What Do I Do When I Get a Cramp in Water?

Getting cramp while running or cycling is unpleasant but can be remedied with a short time-out by stretching the muscles affected. If you often get cramps it would be wise to have the electrolytes in your blood checked. In most cases a magnesium or calcium deficiency is to blame. Whereas an athlete has a firm surface underneath him when he's cycling or running, this is not the case in the water. This is why you should be aware of a few precautionary measures. It's mostly exhaustion and hypothermia which leads to cramp while swimming. This can be dangerous in open waters. During competition you must signal your problems clearly to the escorts or helpers. The easiest way is to raise your hand and wave.

If it happens in training, and you're alone in open water, then try and keep calm no matter what, and keep yourself above water with the simplest but most gentle swimming movements possible.

Cramps occur in the calf muscles, thighs or fingers
Calf cramps are got rid of by stretching the leg, one hand holds the toes and the other hand pushes the knee down. Thigh cramps are best

treated by bending back the lower leg and pulling it up towards one's bottom. Finger cramps are easy to remedy by forming a fist a number of times. There is a certain risk attached to swimming alone in the water. If you do so, then pay attention to the following:

!

- Swim with a neoprene suit which due to its added buoyancy offers a little more safety.
- Choose a swimming route where other swimmers, paddlers, surfers or fishermen are nearby.

7.7 Changeover: Swim-Cycle

Lack of practice in the changeovers in triathlon can lead to large time losses. An athlete who reduces his speed in the final phase of the swim, has already mentally practised the changeover at least once, and has in preparation placed all items where they should be, will manage the change quickly.

The exit from the water is followed by a more or less short run up to the bicycle depending on the length of the changeover zone. This sudden change in the type of movement should be practised now and again in training. Having arrived at the bicycle, now begins the very hectic phase for every athlete: neoprene suit off, goggles and swimming cap off, helmet and shades on, perhaps jersey or shorts, socks on and into the cycling shoes, all in a matter of seconds.

Being too hectic however is no help. When you put on one shoe with your left hand, turn over the start number with the right, you'll probably end up having to start again from scratch. The start number which you attached to the elastic band is for your back.

Particularly important is the **fastening of the helmet** within the changeover zone. Who in all the excitement forgets to do this can be disqualified immediately outside this zone. Another thing, **push** your bike to the end of the changeover zone, or you'll be disqualified here too. When you've managed all this you now must head off in the right gear and concentrate on the road traffic. When cycling obey the rules of the road. The important thing here again: safety comes before time gains!

7.8 Cycling

Exact instructions for cycling training and in competition, including year planning for beginners as well as competitive sportsmen, can be found in the book "The Complete Guide to Triathlon Training". It goes on to look at different aspects of cycling and specific tips for training and competition.

7.8.1 Tips for Racing

In competition you can cycle at a higher speed than in training, with 90 revolutions per minute.

Begin taking drinks before the first signs of thirst appear. Be sure to stay in an aerodynamic position; this also means cycling with the knees moving up and down close to the frame.

Try and cycle with an even, balanced strength effort. This means changing the gear early enough before upward gradients.

Use less effort over the final three kilometres i.e. cycle in lower gears and start loosening up the muscles for running.

Very important! Don't open the chin strap of the helmet until you've entered the changeover zone.

7.8.2 The Particular Demands of the Cycling Race

This second discipline in triathlon, the cycle, sets very high demands on triathletes. These are among others:

Length of Time
Cycling does not only take up the most amount of time in competition but in training too. This is the case for all triathlon distances both for the Olympic Triathlon as well as the Ultra-Distance.

Distance	Olympic		Ultra	
Swimming	1.5 km	18 – 45 min	3.86 km	45 – 120 min
Running	10 km	31 – 60 min	42.2 km	160 – 300 min
Total		49 – 105 min		205 – 420 min
Cycling	40 km	60 – 110 min	180.2 km	254 – 560 min

Food While Cycling
As triathlon is a form of endurance sport composed of three complete endurance disciplines of their own thus requiring both good endurance and a lot of energy, food provision has a very important part to play particularly over the medium and long distances. It's not possible to eat or drink anything while swimming, only fluids are possible while running, but both are possible while cycling. You should always think of this in order to avoid the much dreaded problem of sinking blood sugar level.

How Can I Cut down Air Resistance in the Fairest Way Possible?
As triathlon is an individual and not a team sport, slipstream cycling is forbidden with a few exceptions. Let's make use of the fair methods for better streamlining.

- By using an aerodynamic bike including appropriate wheels.
- By pulling down the handlebars thus having a low, bent over position.
- By keeping the elbows close to the body.
- By wearing tight-fitting clothing.

!

One thing mustn't be forgotten though. One should not sacrifice a comfortable sitting position for all the aerodynamic measures. Handlebars which are down too low can make breathing difficult and cause back problems. Both of these factors have a negative influence on cycling performance and show that there needs to be a compromise reached between the reduction of air resistance and a comfortable sitting position on the bike.

Pedalling Frequency

With this we mean the number of pedal turns in one minute. A rate of 100 means that each foot completed the circular movement 100 times in one minute. When training the rate should lie between 100 - 108. This is almost impossible to manage for someone with little practice. A medium-term increase up to this joint- and muscle-friendly pedalling rate is necessary here. The main cause of serious knee injuries is always a number of revolutions which is too low.

Why Do We Use Eight (Twelve) Gears Out of a Maximum Twelve (Sixteen)?

A chain that runs diagonally causes losses of force which in turn badly affects the speed. In order to avoid this you should heed the following points.

If cycling with the **big front disc** then from the six pinions at the back you should only use four. If there are eight pinions at the back then you should only use six.

When cycling with the **small disc** at the front then you should only use four of the six big pinions at the back, with eight pinions then only six.

Training on a Home Trainer, the 'Roll' or the Ergometer

Anyone who doesn't want to give up cycling in bad weather especially in autumn and winter can still cycle in their living room, in the hall or basement. Suitable are either a home trainer, the so-called 'roll', which is a normal racing bike with the rear wheel running on two rollers, or an ergometer with built-in pulse and heart rate measuring device. The advantages of these are:

- Working people who don't feel like doing their cycling training in the dark can still cycle during the week.
- Cycling training is possible regardless of weather conditions.
- It's possible to check and control load intensity through watt meter, pedalling and pulse rate measurements.

The big disadvantage for many athletes lies in the monotonous nature of this form of training and the enormous sweat formation. These very reasons have kept me from doing this type of training for many years. In the bad seasons I prefer to go running and swimming, and then try in spring to get back into cycling again with a cycling block.

Sitting Problems

A problem which hits many triathletes in the two-week cycling block in spring is the sitting problem. Especially after long distances many cyclists complain of very sore chafing in the perineum area which can get more and more unbearable from day to day. How does one avoid this problem, and if it occurs how does one treat it? By heeding the following tips these unpleasant problems can be avoided:

- Rub cream into the sitting area daily.
- Make sure that the saddle is in correct position i.e.correct for you.
- Increase cycling distances gradually (not from 0 km to 180 km)
- In spring only slowly accustom yourself with the so-called aero-position. This is particularly true for 26 inch wheels where the weight tends to fall more on the front.
- Put on a fresh pair of cycling shorts with a good leather lining every day.
- After each cycling training session wash the sitting area with cold water and rub in cream.

7.9 Changeover: Cycle-Run

After coasting to a stop in the lower gears in the final three kilometres, it's then time to get ready for the change to running - quickly but not in a hectic pace. Come off the bicycle and then enter the changeover zone. Now you may open the strap of the helmet. Many triathletes

Time taking during competition

have ben disqualified for opening it too soon and this is is more than annoying. Those with the cycling shoes in the pedal system go barefoot to their area, park their bicycle and start putting on shoes or jersey.

After this change you should not tear out of the changeover zone like a sprinter but rather calmly try to find your rhythm. This isn't always easy as every athlete is tired after the cycling and is now changing from one type of sport, which is hard on the legs, to yet another one.

This particularly difficult changeover in triathlon should be practised once a week in the final two months before the first competitions. Not at competition speed but in the following way either a short, brisk cycle to be followed immediately with an easy-going run, or a smooth, relaxed cycle to be followed up with a a short, brisk run. This is the only effective way to train for this, the most difficult changeover.

7.10 Running

Before I go any further, here are a few tips for running training and in competition:

- In winter and early spring train basic endurance with long runs at a moderate pace.
- Fartlek 'once a week and occasional fun runs are good for loosening up training somewhat.
- Wear different running shoes alternately.
- For longer runs practise taking drinks.
- Every training unit should be organized as follows: warm-up run, stretching exercises, training unit with easing off and stretching exercises.
- Interval training is not suitable for beginners.
- Number of intervals should be slightly raised every week.
- Confine interval training to 8-12 weeks.
- Be careful, most injuries occur during interval training.
- Run calmly and in a relaxed manner in the triathlon competition.
- Use quick-opening runing shoes.
- Regular intake of drinks is absolutely necessary particularly in hot weather.

!

After swimming and cycling it's now up to us triathletes to go into the run with whatever reserves we still have available. Not only our mental attitude but also the training up to this day should be in gear with this next event. We teeter along for the first steps and the first kilometre. Many triathletes feel as if they're still cycling but with no bike. The speed now when running is not high in comparison to that on the bicycle, on top of this you clearly feel the entire body weight. Definitely a condition which needs a lot of training. Now the time has come for stitches in your side and muscle hardening. Important in this phase is not so much the intake of solids, as that is a strain on the digestive tract, but rather of fluids. As minerals that are now supplied can no longer really be effective, the intake of fluids is now first and foremost to compensate our water balance. This can only be done with water.

Running is the last and the most difficult event, and while running you should try and take in as much of your surroundings as possible - the spectators, the environment and in particular the other runners. This helps to distract you from your own difficulties and makes the time go by more quickly. The same goes for looking forward to the finish, to the helpers, to the cake, to the drinks, to the entire catering etc. If necessary allow yourself little walking breaks at the drink stops. Those with enough strength to run without a break can manage to finish a drink completely with the help of a little tube in the hand.

When the finish is in sight the stride automatically gets longer. The finl spurt is coming up. Run, run smoothly, if possible overtake a competitor or two.

The spectators are clapping. At this moment at the latest every finisher feels like a winner. You, I, all of you, all of us are winners. What a fantastic feeling! Now carbohydrates are necessary which help the body to recover quickly. Drinks are too, those which help to compensate for the loss of minerals. Then come the first stretching exercises for the already beginning phase of regeneration. You see there's still quite a lot to do after the competition.

7.11 Clearing of the Changeover Zone

The clearing of the changeover zone after the competition is important for two reasons. First of all you can pack all the items of equipment together again, from the swimming stuff to the cycling and running gear, and secondly the helpers at the event can now begin their job of taking the zones apart. When you then have all your valuable things stowed away in your car as required you should then devote your time to two factors which will already have an effect on your subsequent condition of performance - nutrition and stretching.

7.12 Nutrition: Food and Drink Before and After Competition

I have already dealt with nutrition in triathlon in detail, and with the various possibilities there are of improving performance through correct eating in the book "The Complete Guide to Triathlon Training". So, at this point I would like to consider several aspects directly relevant to training and competition.

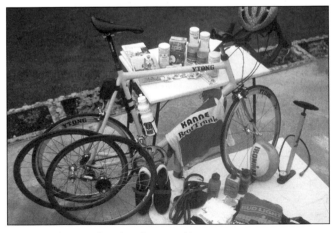

Nutrition - an important factor for performance athletes

Triathletes mostly have a good appetite, particularly in the first few months in the year when basic endurance is being trained. If food is a special enjoyment of life then triathletes can enjoy a lot and often. Of course there are a number of athletes who take delight in their food, don't bother to look if their food is even healthy or suitable for sport in its content. These are lucky people whose appetite and eating habits are sorted out by themselves without them having to pay much attention to quantity and quality. They eat what they like and amazingly enough have no problems.

You can't eat fitness! But a sensible diet helps to improve the effectiveness of training and stabilizes one's health.

Natural products are the best thing for an active person. Not only because they hold the natural balance of vitamins, minerals and trace elements, but also the important enzymes which are necessary for vitamins to take effect.

In aerobic training (lactate rate < 2.0) the necessary energy is supplied in the following proportions: about 48% from carbohydrates, 48% from fatty acids and 4% from proteins.

With anaerobic training the proportion is: about 60% from carbohydrates, 25% from fatty acids and 15% proteins. This means more carbohydrates are burned during long intensive training than in endurance aerobic training. This fact encourages many athletes to try raising the body's carbohydrate reserves (glycogen). One example here is the Saltin diet which is often chosen by many marathon runners. Arthur LYDIARD, the most successful middle and long distance trainer in the world, recommends for this reason the intake of up to 200 g glucose or honey 36 hours before a competition.

Very important for an active person is the composition of his diet. Inadequate nutrition invariably leads to a drop in performance which results in premature tiredness. In a competition this condition then often means giving up.

Carbohydrates play a very important part in a muscle's energy metabolism. They are the 'fuel' for all physical ativities. The body stores carbohydrates mainly in the cell tissue of the muscle or the liver. The better an athlete's training state the bigger these reserves are, and the longer the energy supply is available for his physical activity. For people who play sport it is not so much the simple carbohydrates such as household sugars which are important but rather the so-called complex carbohydrates or multiple sugars. They supply the body with long-lasting energy as well as important minerals and vitamins. Carbohydrates are to be found in: cereals, cereal products, potatoes, pasta and vegetables.

Fats are used up particularly in longer-term endurance performances as is the norm in triathlon, from low to middle intensities. A certain portion of fat is necessary in our diet in order for our body to get essential fatty acids - linol acids - which it can not produce itself. Having said this, triathletes can manage with a relatively small proportion of fats in their diet. For this reason one should watch out for the so-called hidden fats. These are present in meat, sausage, chocolate, cheese, sauces, eggs, all foods fried in breadcrumbs, pancakes, cakes and desserts and chips (French fries).

Triathletes should be particularly sure to eat enough **proteins** as regular training increases the body's protein requirements. A danger of having a protein deficiency exists due to the fact that only fats and carbohydrates as sources of energy can be stored in our body, but not proteins. An inadequate protein intake can thus lead to muscle cramp, strains, less resistance to infection, reduction in concentration, in co-ordination, in one's general readiness for performance, in activity and in the joy of living.

The greater need for protein relates to the building of new muscles and because a triathlete has a higher proportion of muscles the 'maintenance' of these muscles.

As regards the breaking down of our nutritive elements Dr. med. STRUNZ recommends an intake percentage for carbohydrate/fats/ proteins of 60/20/20. As few people can understand this exactly he has other clearer advice:

As much protein as possible, little fat, and the proportion of carbohydrate sorts itself out automatically!

In order to reach a sufficient daily intake of proteins in our diet, one must not only be sure to take in enough protein altogether but to have the balance of animal and vegetable proteins. One should also pay attention to the following favourable protein combinations:

- Cereals + pulse vegetables
- Corn + beans
- Potato + egg, milk, meat, fish
- Bread + sausagemeat,cheese, milk, egg.

Vitamins

Physical strain through training does not only lead to a high use of energy. The human constituents, carbohydrates, proteins and fats, can only be absorbed when vitamins are supplied at the same time. Fast foods which above all are lacking in vitamins and minerals are then anything but necessary for an active person. Particularly important are the vitamins A_1, B_1, B_2, B_6, B_{12}, C and E. Vitamins are also suitable for fighting colds and flu'.

Minerals

Mineral elements are imperative for muscle work. As numerous minerals are lost through sweat formation, these losses must be compensated for with food intake. Mineral deficiency can take the form of cramps and a general drop in performance. As there is no 'storage space' for minerals either, a continual compensation is recommended through fresh and mixed foods.

7.12.2 Drinking for Triathlon

a) During Training

The intake and output of fluids is very significant for all endurance sportsmen in particular for triathletes, and this relationship can even be of vital significance in the warm and hot time of the year. A loss of 2-3 litres per hour is possible on hot days. If these fluid losses are not constantly compensated for this means that both the blood and the entire body is missing out on water. The blood gets thicker and as a result cannot carry out its transport duties at a satisfactory level.

Endurance performance already suffers at a loss of 2%. The simultaneously occurring feeling of thirst signals to us "drink, drink, drink". Who ignores this feeling and does not take in fluids at this stage risks experiencing nausea, psychological disturbances, lack of motor coordination, which is indicated through swaying and

staggering instead of running. These symptoms are completely avoidable and occur at a loss of water of approx. 6%, and unfortunately these are the pictures that are always shown by the media. That even mature, professional triathletes in Hawaii don't take the time to supply their body with sufficient fluids is something which I just can't understand. They are endangering their health with this foolishness. This can't be the point of this sport! Sweating unfortunately means the loss of vital mineral elements which have to be tanked up again as quickly as possible. Not every mineral is the same, and for this reason athletes should look for water with the highest content possible of magnesium (Mg > 100 mg/l), calcium (Ca > 200 mg/l) as well as the lowest possible content of sodium (Na < 50 mg/l). For regulating the loss of body fluids in training and in competition I and, as I know from many letters - a great number of other triathletes have found the following drink mix to promote one's performance:

1 measure of 'Brottrunk' + 1 measure of apple juice

This mixture replaces both the minerals lost through sweat, as well as the Vitamin C which is also gone, and leads to a balance in the mineral 'household' again. At the same time there is an increase in oxygen partial pressure. Linked to this is an improved metabolism which in turn causes a natural improvement in performance. For hard training, or competitions, an intake of Brottrunk, a lactic acid fermented drink, brings about better blood circulation and removal of the toxic tissue acid. As a consequence you have neither aching muscles nor cramps. A mixture of pure apple juice and mineral water is another rational way to replace lost fluids.

The much praised ready mineral drinks are often so concentrated that they lead to a compulsory break from training and competition with diarrhoea. For hot temperatures it is wise to drink 0.5-1l fluid even before training. Mineral substitutes on prescription are often necessary in two areas, according to Dr. Ulrich STRUNZ after many years of tests with competitive athletes. These are for magnesium and iron.

More details of this and of triathletes' blood values can be found in "The Complete Guide to Triathlon Training" from p. 216 onwards.

b) During Competition

In general all situations which occur in competition should be tested in training. This includes above all drink and food intake. Therefore never try out something new in competition. The chances of experiments going right at competition load intensity are relatively slim.

The following can be recommended as regards food intake:
Before every event you are informed about the solid foods being distributed on the routes. However this is only necessary for competitions above the Olympic Distance. If you are not familiar with these foods then it is better to bring your own food e.g. energy bars in the pocket of the cycling jersey or stuck to the frame of the bike.
The provision of your own drinks must be organised before the competition.

!

Helpful in this respect is knowledge of
● where the feeding stations are
● the points where you can get your own foods
● the types of drinks being offered
● in what order the drinks are offered

You should have two full bottles in your bottle holder. If there are points at which one's own items can be taken, and you have your own assistant, then make use of this. If your own drinks are finished then only take drinks which you are familiar with. If this is not possible then I would advise you above all to take water and bananas. You can't go wrong there.

Be careful when it's very hot and your body needs a lot of fluids as a result, one beaker-full of an unfamiliar, highly concentrated mineral drink can be enough to stimulate your bowel to such an extreme that you are forced to take unpleasant time-outs.

Eating Before the Competition
What's normally frowned upon brings a lot of advantages on the day of competition. What you need here is a light breakfast low in roughage, so as not to put any unnecessary strain on the digestive system and to fulfil the prerequirement for quick energy supplies in competition.

This is possible with the intake of white bread with honey or sugar beet syrup, fruit and fruit juices + Brottrunk.

On days when it's expected to be hot, or for long distances, take an extra 0.5 l drink half an hour before the start.

Drinking and Eating After Training or Competition
The time needed for you to be top fit again after training or competition depends among other things to a large extent on food and drink you now take. After this effort it is recommended to take carbohydrates and fluids. Fluids rich in carbohydrates, soups, diluted fruit juices and Brottrunk are all very suitable here. After this your store of carbohydrates should be filled up with solid foods such as bread, rice, pasta, potatoes, oat flakes and others. As fat only delays the intake of carbohydrates foods rich in fat e.g. meat and sausage products, full dairy products, chocolate and cake are not suitable. In the first few hours after the competition pressure you should do without foods with a high roughage content as these make you feel full, thus preventing the further intake of carbohydrates.

Triathlon and Luxuries

It is well-known that a huge of endurance athletes go for cakes and sweet things. The reason for this is the drop in the blood sugar levels after a long sport activity. Instead of aiming towards such 'luxuries' as chocolate, cake, sweets, ice cream, Coke, lemonades, coffee, black tea or alcoholic drinks - the 'empty' joule/calorie foods - it's more advisable to satisfy these 'cravings' with highly nutritious foods e.g. fruit, dried fruit and wholemeal cakes. Coffee and black teas have the further disadvantage in that they have a diuretic effect and deprive the athlete of two basic elements: firstly water which is a solvent and a means of transport, and secondly the mineral elements which have dissolved in this water.

Triathlon and 'Alcohol'

Alcohol has both short-term and long-term negative effects on a person's organism, and in particularly on the organism of a triathlete. Following load-intensive training or a competition alcohol delays the new build-up of energy reserves in the recovery phase. This in turn leads to a more or less significant impairment (depending on the amount of alcohol involved) in a triathlete's performance development. Even the argument that beer contains a lot of carbohydrates is not watertight, as fruit juices contain these nutrients in much higher proportions. As an organic solvent alcohol hinders the intake of nutrients, in particular vitamins and mineral elements.

A regular consumption does therefore not fit into a performance-oriented diet.

7.13 Flexibility and Stretching - in Co-operation with the Physiotherapist Carmen Aschwer

Flexibility and suppleness is the degree of movement within a joint (e.g. knee joint) or several joints (spinal column). The extent of the movement depends on the stretchability of the elastic structures, i.e. the muscles, ligaments, tendons, form of joint and muscle strength.

Human skeletal muscles are made up of thousands of muscle fibres. These are as thin as a hair and can be from 10-15 cm in length depending on the size of the muscle. We generally distinguish between two types of muscle fibre, firstly the 'phase' muscles or 'white fibres'. These are easily prone to fatigue and weakening and are necessary for locomotion and aiming movement. Secondly we have the 'tonic' muscles or the 'red muscle fibres'. These are slow to tire but are prone to shortening and are responsible for a person's statics and support movement. Through certain forms of load the proportion of these muscle fibres can change. Triathlon and marathon athletes for example have over 90% red muscle fibres in the frontal thigh muscles, i.e. those which are slow to tire.

7.13.1 Why Should Triathletes Do Stretching?

As a triathlete's 'tonic' muscles are in demand for several hours and this type of muscle fibre, prone to shortening stretching, must thus become an important part of training. Changes in muscle stretchability can cause injuries in the muscle and muscle insertion. Furthermore they prevent a person's statics as well as having an unfavourable effect on the pressure load in joints.

7.13.2 Consequences of Careless Stretching

If the muscles are not stretched sufficiently then one can expect to have a reduction in development of strength and speed. This in turn will lead to performance deficits. The aim of muscle stretching is to restore the normal muscle length and to achieve a balance between the different muscles worked on, the performing ones (agonist) and the slowing down ones (antagonist). To improve the elasticity of muscles it is necessary to actively warm them up. Active means here a warm-up run and not just the well-meant rubbing in with muscle fluid. With regard to one's sport performance capacity stretching exercises have the following purpose:

- Preparation for physical activity
- Improvement in muscle blood flow and meatabolism
- Increase in stride length when running
- Maintenance of the normal muscle length
- Improvement in technique
- Psychological relaxation
- To convey a better perception of one's own body
- Reduction of the risk of getting muscle and joint injuries
- Regeneration after intensive training and competition loads.

7.13.3 When Is Stretching Necessary?

The stretching phase should be a permanent part of every training session. This means after the warm-up phase and at the very end of the training unit to be exact. The purpose of it is to bring the tired and shortened muscles back to normal size again.

Furthermore you must take into account that only stretching exercises which are done regularly will bring the desired success.

Be careful! In cold weather and early in the morning you are not as flexible as in warm temperatures or in the evening. Young people are more able to stretch than older peoples. However with regular training a good flexibility can be maintained even up to old age.

7.13.4 How Does One Do Stretching?

There are different types of stretching. For triathletes the passive-static stretching is the most effective. Stretching exercises are principally carried out in the contrary direction to the function of the particular muscle. This is the only way of restoring the normal length in the muscle.

Heed the following **principle** when carrying out all stretching exercises:

Having taken up the appropriate stretching position the stretch is then minimally intensified in the direction of the arrow while still in this position. In the process there is an increase in resistance which becomes noticeable through a 'stretched sensation' .

The following points must also be considered:
- A pulling sensation is allowed.
- Pain is to be avoided.
- Calm, even breathing throughout the entire stretching exercise.
- Stretch should last 15 - 30 seconds per exercise.
- 2 - 4 repetitions
- Carry out loosening - up exercises between the stretching exercises.
- Only stretch muscles, and not ligaments or tendons as ligaments, have a supportive function, and tendons a force-transmitting function to fulfil.

There are many variations in the area of stretching exercises. Some examples are shown below. Anyone who wishes to find out more information on this should refer to the following book: SCHMIDT/ HILLEBRECHT - Stretching and Strengthening Exercises (see Glossary).

Swimming

1. Stretching of the lateral neck
   muscles

Bend your head to one side, tilt it to the front and then turn your head to the 'stretch' side. Tense the arm that is hanging down toward the floor.

2. Stretching of the upper arm
   muscles and muscles of the broad
   of the back

Take the upper arm up behind the back and with the other hand pull the elbow further towards the other shoulder.

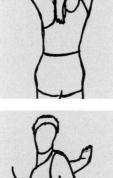

3. Stretching of the pectoral muscles

Stand sideways in the door frame or at the wall. Then turn the upper body away from the side to be stretched, transferring your weight to the front in the process.

4. Stretching of the lateral trunk muscles
Lift the arm up to the side and pull it over the head to the other side

5. Stretching of the front shoulder muscles, pectoral muscles and muscles of the inner upper arm
In an upright position put your hands together behind your back, pressing your shoulder blades together while doing so. Raise your almost fully outstretched arms as far back and up as possible. The shortening of these muscles makes the front crawl difficult.

Stretching exercises for cycling and running

1. Stretching of the calf muscles
Assume stride position. Keep the rear leg stretched pressing the heels on the floor. Now transfer the weight to the front leg and bend the front knee.
A shortening of the calf muscle means that correct rolling of the foot, which is so important for running, is not possible.

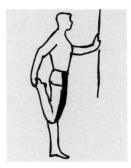

2. Stretching of the frontal thigh muscles
Stand in an upright position, take the heel to the buttocks, making sure that the hips remain stretched and no hollow back appears.

3. Stretching of the hip flexing muscles
Assume one-legged knee stand and place the leg to be stretched as far back as possible. Now try to guide the hip down and towards the front.
Important:
A shortening of the hip flexing muscles reduces the stride length.

4. Stretching of the inner thigh
   muscles (adductors)
Extend the leg to be stretched out to the side and try to get down as low as possible toward the floor.

5. Stretching of the rear thigh muscles
1st possibility:
Get into supine position. Put your hands around the leg to be stretched at the back of the knee and then bring the lower leg to a stretched position.

2nd possibility:
In an upright position place the heel of the leg to be stretched upon a chair or other suitable item (stairs, table, fence, tree). While both legs are being stretched the upper body is bent forward.

6. Stretching of the posterior muscles
In a supine position pull the leg to be stretched as close as possible toward the body. In this position then bring it to the side.

7. Stretching of the pectoral muscles and lateral trunk muscles
Get into supine position, bend the knees and place the arms beside the head. 'Kip' the legs in this position to one side towards the floor. Shoulders are to be on the floor at all times.

7.14 Prevention of Injuries

The commonly held opinion that triathlon makes you 'hardy', offers a great number of advantages for your health, strengthens the body's immune system through stress-free training as well as stabilising your psyche has often been confirmed in numerous medical studies. This is true for the area of mass sports: Highly performance-oriented athletes who train several times a week or even a day and have concrete goals ahead of them demand a lot from their bodies. Working at a high load level may thus make our bodies more vulnerable with possible problems in adapting or overuse injuries. This is due to the differing adaptabilities of the various organic systems following repeated loads.

Our breathing, metabolism, digestion and fluid 'household' are all very quick to adapt to repeated loads, whereas our cardiovacular system is somewhat slower. These time delays are even longer in the case of muscles. Extremely slow to adapt on the other hand are our ligaments, tendons and joints.

On account of this fact performance-oriented triathletes may find adaptation problems, or even injuries, appearing which can be avoided with appropriate treatment.

Note: I am not a doctor and not qualified to give medical advice. But seeing as I have been running for almost twenty years and doing triathlon for fifteen years, I have experienced a series of typical athlete problems in my sporting environment. The following chapter is to be considered as a helpful tip from one triathlete to another and not as professional medical advice. However should an athlete be having any doubts whatsoever about an injury, a visit to the doctor is obviously advisable.

I myself have to say that I have managed to stay injury-free in the fifteen years of systematic training for triathlon, with the exception of a few minor strains (as a result of insufficient stretching) and two falls from a bike.

Triathlon is a form of endurance sport which helps in the strengthening of the cardiovascular system and of many groups of muscles. However a person who wishes to start with systematic training after years of sport abstinence should consult a doctor beforehand. It's important here to seek a doctor who has a positive attitude to sport.

However it can even happen with these very doctors that on hearing the word 'triathlon' they have visions of the media-effective Ironman Hawaii Triathlon, and regard the beginner with a certain amount of scepticism. Fill your doctor in in this respect i.e. that a triathlon begins with the beginner or novice distances of 500 m swimming, 20 km cycling and 5 km running and even these distances require regular training. Although the risks of sport injuries are relatively slim in triathlon, nobody is completely immune. A total **break from training** is necessary with feverish colds, influenza and stomach bugs. When the infection has passed it's advisable to rest for another two or three days and then begin again with calm, light training.

Prophylactic Measures, Prevention of Injuries
Anyone who sticks to a few simple, plausible principles in training and in competition can do a lot to avoid having any injuries at all even in intensive phases. Included here are the following:

- well-fitting shoes with the right shock absorbency
- do not increase training kilometres in running by more than 10% per week
- always follow up hard days of training with a relaxed day or one free of training
- carry out flexibility and stretching exercises regularly
- never cycle without a cycling helmet
- increase the training volume and then the training intensity

A triathlete has a unique advantage. Even with problems in e.g. running, he is still able to carry out cycling and swimming training. This is similar with the other sports. Training impediments in one discipline can mostly be compensated for by more intensive training in the other disciplines.

Apart from this the good old remedies 'rest and recovery', or ' Dr. Time and Dr. Care', often help remarkably quickly, effectively as well as being very reasonable in price! Should certain problems occur however the first thing to do is reduce training intensity or stop training completely. And if minor injuries still appear, then maybe the following advice from the area of sport practice offer certain help.

Blisters

Blisters are a gathering of fluid between two layers of skin as a result of friction. They may be a result of badly fitting running shoes (size, width) or socks rubbing.

Vaseline and talcum powder on the approriate areas can be of help here. Furthermore the shoe's 'size' can be varied e.g. by tying the shoelaces differently, by using thicker or thinner insoles or socks.

Grazes

Grazes occur mostly from cycling falls. They must be cleaned off immediately. A special spray gives the first instant treatment. Often lurking behind these light, slightly bleeding grazes is the risk of an infection through tetanus germs. One should always be vaccinated against tetanus.

Stitches in the Side

If running rhythm is not in keeping with breathing rhythm then you get a stitch in your side. It can be also a result of running too quickly, or running with a full stomach.

No matter what the reason begin to run more slowly and breathe out slowly and properly. Another way of getting rid of this unpleasant condition when running is to reduce running speed for approx. 30 seconds; with a stitch on the right-hand side breathe out when the left foot touches down, and for a stitch on the left then breathe out on the right foot. As an extra supportive measure fold your hands over your head push elbows back and breathe deeply from the stomach.

Muscle Soreness

It used to be thought that muscle soreness had something to do with the formation of lactic acid during the production of energy. Nowadays we know for sure that muscle soreness leads to a tearing of the small so-called Z-discs (microtraumas). The breakdown and build-up again of the muscle takes three to four days. In this process the muscle is supposed to strengthen itself at the weak points with additional tiny muscle fibres. A reduction of muscle soreness and this breakdown can only come about by means of a movement to enhance blood flow and not through strain. Even better of course is to prevent the occurrence of this unpleasant conditon in the first place. This is possible through the intake of Brottrunk before and after physical effort. It's this preventative measure which has kept me free from aching muscles in the last ten years.

Hardening of the Calf Muscles
Triathletes who only run on the tips of their toes, or on the balls of their feet, have a typical track running style. This often leads to tension in the calf muscles. The style of running must be altered in such a way that the heel touches down first and then the entire foot is 'rolled'. This tension ceases completely after this.

Cramps
Muscle cramp is an extremely unpleasant matter for triathletes. It involves a very painful contraction of the muscle. The best way of getting rid of this cramp is to stretch the muscles in the opposite direction. Massages and cooling sprays are not effective here.

Muscle cramp may have a number of causes such as the overuse of a muscle, underuse of a muscle, deficiency of electrolytes, problems with blood flow in a specific area which may have been caused by infection, varicose veins or simply by wearing shoes which are too tight. Generally speaking a link which is too weak in the 'muscle-chain' is most likely to be overstrained. Or another cause is the incorrect position for certain axes of movement e.g. in the case of curvature of the spine, scoliotic pelvis, knock-knees, rounded back or club-foot. Due to the various alternative 'lever' positions, we have a clear multiple load of a certain muscle in particular. This muscle will always tend to cramp earlier than the other normally-loaded muscles. The much dreaded thigh cramps can be triggered off by worn-out shoes. In order to avoid this happening the running shoe is very important. However an additional cause of cramp can be a lack of electrolytes which has come about within a specific part of the muscle itself.

Those electrolytes or mineral salts which are important for muscle effort are sodium, magnesium, calcium, potassium, phosphorous and chlorine. If these elements are lost from the body through sweat and not replaced again soon enough through the intake of drinks, then the muscle loses its ability to contract under control. The consequence is a long-term contraction, a cramp. This unfortunate state of affairs however can be avoided by means of correct nutrition. I have managed this now for over 10 years, despite many long competitions and unbearably hot temperatures. And how? Through the regular intake of Brottrunk.

Insomnia

Another problem often arises in connection with insomnia, strong palpitations. Both problems are symptoms of 'overtraining', i.e. when the sports load is too high. You must now review your training over the last few weeks. Firstly you must pay attention to the sport quality or intensity, and secondly the quantity of the sports load. Furthermore you must examine the entire surrounding factors as regards too much overall strain in working, private and sports life.

Being Vulnerable to Infections

For those triathletes who train at performance or high performance levels the immune system has often, or always, to be running at top form. If an infection comes about then the body just can't manage this any more. Sport performances get worse and worse and as an athlete you feel totally drained. Unfamiliar days of rest are what's needed now. Even for endurance sportsmen two to three colds a year are normal. An athlete who is often coughing, sneezing or is hoarse should think about their immune system. Many colds are a sign that the body's defence system is weaker than it should be. The function of our immune system is to recognise germs and make them harmless. As well as this it must rid the body of very old or damaged cells and destroy degenerated cells. For performance and high performance athletes, with their intensive physical activity, there are significantly more damaged or destroyed cells to be disposed of. As a result the immune system can be overworked and overstrained thus allowing more colds and infections to set in. This is a clear sign of overtraining.

How Can I Stop Possible Colds and Infections?

It's extremely important to avoid hypothermia from wet or sweat-soaked clothing. This is possible with suitable headwear, warm sports clothing and an immediate change of clothing after training.

Overtraining

If there is a sudden clear drop in performance in competition or training without being organically ill we then refer to 'overtraining'. I have already described in detail the typical symptoms and the many measures necessary to get out of this situation of overtraining in the book "The Complete Guide to Triathlon Training" from page 39 onwards. The most important factor is that something is done to combat this unsatisfactory state of performance immediately after it has been confirmed.

Achilles Tendon Trouble

The achilles tendon connects the calf muscles to the heel. An inflammation in this region can be described as a dull, sometimes sharp pain along the outer side of the achilles tendon. Combined with this is often a hardening of the lower calf muscles. After training it is wise to use a cold compress on the area. As well as this the appropriate running shoe should be lined with a piece of foam rubber 15-20 mm thick, or should have a 5 mm thick cork insole in both running and walking shoes. Careful stretching of the calves is advisable every day. Running training should only be taken up again carefully when the pain has subsided completely. If you feel strain on your achilles tendon when cycling then check the saddle height. The recommendations for treatment of the above-mentioned revolve around the same principle as for the knee pain below.

Knee Pain

Pain in the knee is not unusual when cycling or running. The most common reason for this is over-intensive training, or when the training volume has been increased too quickly. Cold temperatures are also noticed in the knee. For this one can only recommend warm clothing. Particularly hard on the knees are high gears when cycling and downhill phases when running. Knee problems also tend to hit newcomers to sport, or athletes who have had a long break.

As long as there are no real injuries to the bone the physician Dr. Ernst van AAKEN, also known as the 'Pope of running', recommends using moist bandages during the night for inflammation of the achilles tendon, knee problems, **periostitis**. These bandages are easy to make, just take a damp, cold towel, a dry towel, covered with 'cling-film' and an elastic bandage. This dressing promotes better blood flow for approx. eight hours thus enhancing the healing process.

Triathletes with knee problems should particularly heed the following points:

- Choose running shoes carefully.
- Calm build-up of training; avoid increasing the training volume too quickly.
- Regular stretching.
- Constant checking of running technique.
- Cycle with a pedalling frequency of approx. 100 rpm.
- Have warm knee covering for cold temperatures.

Back pain

The cause of back pain with triathletes can be both the aerodynamic, bent position on the bicycle as well as the strain from high and intensive volumes of running. When a lot is demanded of the back muscles it can result in slow development of the abdominal muscles. As a preventative measure performance athletes should not only do flexibility and stretching exercises for the well worn out back muscles but also for the abdominal muscles which can take up to 40% of the upper body's weight. What counts in cycling is not to always lie over the handlebars in the typical triathlon position, but rather to sit most of the time in a more upright position in training. In the early year it's a good idea to continue cycling with a higher handlebar position. Several athletes sing the praises of a bicycle frame with 'swing' for back problems. The saddle here is attached onto a suspended pinion thus taking some pressure off the back muscles.

If the back problems occur mainly while running, then you must heed three factors: The correct shoes, a reduction in running intensity and a reduction in running volume.

If you've been having pain for a long while then you ought to visit a sport orthopaedic doctor. He will examine you for defects in the spinal column, scoliotic pelvis, hollow back or for differing leg lengths.

Strains, Bruises and Swelling

According to Dr. van AAKEN these minor complaints for a triathlete should also be treated with moist dressings over night.

Diarrhoea

Diarrhoea in training, but particularly in competition, is an unfortunate thing to have and prevents every athlete from coming near to his performance limit. If it occurs during a competition it may either be a direct result of untested nutrition but it could just as likely be psychological. The aspect regarding nutrition is dealt with in the chapter "Nutrition". Those athletes who put themselves under intense pressure before a competition (I have to make the qualification for the National Championship, European Championship, the World Championship or Hawaii, I must be first or second in my age category, I must....., I must......,) often don't even notice that they are no longer doing sport for the sake of fun or for exercise but are becoming a slave to the sport instead. It's often the case that diarrhoea then occurs for no apparent reason and the athlete misses out on his personal goal as well. However isn't this self-made problem a reasonable explanation, indeed the perfect reason, to give to friends, relatives and acquaintances for one's failure in sport competitions? No, it definitely is not. What you have to do in this case is to look at things rationally, get to the root of the problem and solve it yourself.

7.15 Regeneration

Two regenerative measures within our triathlon cycle have been looked at so far - food and drink after the competition and flexibility and stretching exercises. The whole idea of regeneration is for the athlete to recover as quickly as possible. An athlete who regenerates fast is soon able to take up his normal training workload and therefore has a higher performance capacity than an athlete who requires a longer regeneration phase.

Further measures which help towards fast regeneration after our 'triathlon competition:

● Relaxed cycle of 10 km
● Very easy run of 2-3 km
● Look for a jacuzzi, sauna or regeneration bath

Obviously training in the next coming weeks will be reduced both in volume and intensity in comparison to normal training. Plan for more rest days than usual. As swimming and cycling are not as hard on the body as running, it makes sense for triathletes to concentrate preferably on the first two.

Through these measures the risk of overtraining is reduced. Then begins the build-up again to the next triathlon competition, which after sufficient regeneration commences with stage 1 of our triathlon cycle, i.e. training. The next goal, the next calculated risk, can thus be set and worked on.

Surprisingly enough this constant cycle keeps on showing new, interesting aspects of our many-side sport, and I wish you the very best of luck with it.

Whether the cycle is repeated once, three times or even 10-15 times in the next year, and whether one, two, three, ten or in my case fifteen years are added on to this is entirely your decision. I can only guarantee that I would not like to have missed out on any of the numerous sportive, interhuman or touristic experiences that I have had thanks to all these fascinating competitions.

Triathlon was and still is a great personal enrichment for me.

I wish exactly the same for you!

Literature

Aaken, E. van: Das van Aaken Lauflehrbuch.
    Meyer & Meyer Verlag, Aachen 1997.
Aschwer, H.: Mein Abenteuer Hawaii-Triathlon.
    Meyer & Meyer Verlag, Aachen (out of print).
Aschwer, H.: Handbuch für Triathlon.
    Meyer & Meyer Verlag, Aachen 1995.
Aschwer, H.: Triathlon-Training. Vom Jedermann zum Ironman.
    Meyer & Meyer Verlag, Aachen 1996.
Aschwer, H.: Ironman Der Hawaii-Triathlon.
    Meyer & Meyer Verlag, Aachen 1997.
Cooper, H.: Dr. Coopers Gesundheitsprogramm.
    Droemar Verlag 1994.
Diem, Carl-J.: Tips für Laufanfänger.
    Meyer & Meyer Verlag, Aachen 1997.
Galloway, J.: Richtig laufen mit Galloway.
    Meyer & Meyer Verlag, Aachen 1996.
Hahn, K.: 60 Marathonstrecken hat eine Stunde.
    Jahn & Ernst Verlag 1998.
Hottenrott, K.: Duathlontraining.
    Meyer & Meyer Verlag, Aachen 1997.
Schmidt/Hillebrecht: Übungsprogramme zur Dehn- und Kräftigungs-
    gymnastik. Meyer & Meyer Verlag 1996.
Steffny, M.: Marathon-Training.
    Schmidt Verlag, Mainz 1994.

Photos:

P. 14: G. Anderwald
P. 20: S. Aschwer
P. 22: S. Aschwer
P. 26: H. Aschwer
P. 30: Krabo
P. 32: H. Aschwer
P. 35: H. Aschwer
P. 36: arena
P. 38: Krabo
P. 44: Habo
P. 45: Sandra Schreiber
P. 49 left: Hestia Pharma GmbH
P. 49 right: Polar Electro GmbH
P. 60: G. Mangold
P. 64 above: S. Aschwer
P. 64 down: H. Nowak
P. 65: S. Aschwer
P. 69: Action Sports
P. 70: Action Sports
P. 74: S. Aschwer
P. 76: Action Sports
P. 77: S. Aschwer
P. 81: H. Kaldewei
P. 100: Carmen Aschwer

The Fascination of Sport!

Volume 1
Steffen Grosse
Fascination Triathlon
Training – Performance –
Success
Video

Through training to performance, through performance
to success. In this videos
Steffen Grosse will give you
training advice and share the
benefit of his experience.
Using vividly detailed images
coaches and sportspeople
will be clearly shown successful training methods for the
three basic sports (Vol. 1).

VHS – Volume 1: 61 min
ISBN 1-84126-033-9

NTSC – Volume 1: 61 min
ISBN 1-84126-038-X

£ 17.95 UK/$ 29.- US/
$ 39.95 CDN

Volume 2
Steffen Grosse
Fascination Triathlon
Training – Performance –
Success
Video

Further training methods with
advice on recuperation and
equipment (Vol. 2).

VHS – Volume 2: 54 min
ISBN 1-84126-034-7

NTSC – Volume 2: 54 min
ISBN 1-84126-039-8

£ 17.95 UK/$ 29.- US/
$ 39.95 CDN

Volume 1+2 (Kombi)

VHS –
Vol. 1: 61 min + Vol. 2: 54 min
ISBN 1-84126-049-5

NTSC –
Vol. 1: 61 min + Vol. 2: 54 min
ISBN 1-84126-050-9

£ 33.95 UK/$ 54.95 US/
$ 74.95 CDN

MEYER & MEYER Verlag | Von-Coels-Straße 390 | D-52080 Aachen, Germany | Fax ++49 (0)2 41/9 58 10-10

MEYER
& MEYER
SPORT